A TEACHING COMPANION TO

LEMMON'S BEGINNING LOGIC

A TEACHING COMPANION TO
LEMMON'S BEGINNING LOGIC

George F. Schumm
The Ohio State University

Hackett Publishing Company, Inc.

Indianapolis . Cambridge

ISBN 0-915144-65-4

Library of Congress Catalog Card Number 78-51926

Second printing

1980

For further information, please address

Hackett Publishing Company, Inc.

P.O. Box 55573

Indianapolis, Indiana 46205

Printed in the United States of America

TABLE OF CONTENTS

TABLE OF CONTENTS (cont.)

III. SOLUTIONS TO SELECTED **SUPPLEMENTARY** EXERCISES

Chapter 1

Chapter 2

Chapter 3

Chapter 4

PREFACE (To the Instructor)

E. J. Lemmon's BEGINNING LOGIC is a minor classic among logic texts, and its reprinting by Hackett Publishing Company is most welcome. Despite a number of shortcomings, the book has much useful life left in it. It has been my experience, in fact, that even some of its defects can be quite instructive and turned to good advantage in the classroom.

This COMPANION is not an instructor's manual, nor yet a full-fledged study guide. It was drafted initially in response to three common complaints: (1) that Lemmon's text does not contain enough exercises, (2) that the exercises are sometimes too "textbookish" and (3) that no solutions are provided. It became increasingly clear, however, as I attempted to formulate certain exercises and solutions that some commentary on the text would be essential if confusion was to be avoided. The result is primarily an exercise booklet, with exercises ranging from the simple to the challenging, and with an emphasis on the analysis of fairly realistic English arguments. Solutions are provided for perhaps 25-30% of these exercises and those in the text. But there is also included a discussion of Lemmon's use of such key terms as 'argument', 'premiss', 'assumption', 'conclusion', 'proof', 'rest upon' and the like (pp. 1-15), derived rules of derivation (pp. 71-3), and the justification for studying the material conditional (pp. 81-9), brief mention of switching circuits (p. 28) and many-valued, free and modal logics (pp. 41-7), and a sprinkling of comments and suggestions. This material would all be greatly expanded should this COMPANION later be turned into a full-fledged study guide.

Use of the COMPANION is straightforward: after finishing each section of the text, the student should read the corresponding section of this document and try the supplementary exercises (if any).

My thanks to Ronald Laymon, Bill Lycan, George Pappas and Stewart Shapiro for some nice suggestions. I am especially grateful to John Corcoran, State University of N.Y. at Buffalo, whose extensive and perceptive comments in connection with an earlier draft convinced me of the need to include the material on pp. 1-15--though I fear he'll find it all too brief.

William Hackett forbade my entitling this document 'LEMMON AID', lest a few readers be offended, but confessed that Lemmon would probably have enjoyed the conceit.

This COMPANION was written with the needs of
my own students in mind, but is offered in the hope
that it might prove useful to others as well. I would
appreciate any comments, criticisms or suggestions
the reader may have. If the response to this version
justifies the time and effort required, this document
will later be expanded into a much longer, full-fledged
commentary and study guide.

I. SUPPLEMENTARY EXERCISES AND MATERIAL

Chapter 1, sec. 1

1   Lemmon warns on p. 2 that he'll use the terms 'sound' and 'valid' interchangeably. Most logicians would use here only the latter term, calling an argument 'sound' only if it were valid <u>and</u> had all true premisses. Lemmon has no special term for arguments sound in this other sense. It's important that this and other terminological matters be kept in mind if you've had a previous introduction to logic or if you consult another logic text.

Chapter 1, sec. 2

1   Pp. 8-12 are among the most important in the entire text and should be read several times. You may find these pages puzzling, however, especially in light of what was said back in sec. 1. One reason is that Lemmon uses such key terms as 'argument', 'premiss', 'assumption', 'conclusion' and 'soundness' in several different senses (and without warning that he's doing so). Another is that for stylistic reasons or for reasons having to do with the organization of the text, he sometimes uses one notion where, strictly speaking, he should be using some related notion. Let me try to forestall some of these potential confusions by sketching the "big picture" on which Lemmon is operating. You should read this through a couple of times now. If some of it seems a little hard to grasp, don't get overly concerned. On rereading, after you've finished Chapter 2, it should all seem a lot more familiar and may serve to tie together many of the concepts you'll have been studying.

ARGUMENTS. On p. 1, the term 'argument' is used to refer to a complex of propositions, one of which (the <u>conclusion</u>) is claimed to follow from the others (the <u>premisses</u>). Thus, in the following argument

(A)   All women are mortal; Xanthippe is a woman; therefore, Xanthippe is mortal.

the first two propositions constitute the premisses, and the third the conclusion.

By 'proposition' Lemmon means <u>what is expressed</u> by a declarative sentence, where this is to be distinguished from the sentence itself (p. 6). Thus, for example, the first premiss of A is not the <u>sentence</u> 'All women are mortal' but the proposition that all women are mortal--the proposition expressed by that sentence. Not all logicians would follow Lemmon on this score, and would choose instead to think of an argument as a complex of sentences. Whether one should go one way or the other is an important issue in the philosophy of logic, but need not detain us here. The distinction between sentences and propositions plays no crucial role in Lemmon's text or in the study of logic generally, looming large only when one turns to worry over the philosophical underpinnings of the subject.

On the bottom of p. 1, Lemmon divides arguments into those that are <u>sound</u> (or <u>valid</u>) and those that are <u>unsound</u> (or <u>invalid</u>). An argument is sound if its conclusion follows from (is entailed by, is a consequence of) its premisses in the sense that it's <u>impossible</u> for all the premisses to be true and (at the same time) the conclusion false. (An argument is unsound if it is not sound.) The interest in sound arguments thus arises from the fact that if one accepts all the premisses of such an argument, one is thereby committed (on pain of inconsistency) to its conclusion.

DEDUCTIONS. Often, however, logicians use the term 'argument' in another sense--to refer to a piece of reasoning leading from a set of assumptions to a final conclusion, and including all the intermediate conclusions gotten along the way. Within pp. 8-11, Lemmon calls such a piece of reasoning 'an argument', 'a total argument', 'a piece of reasoning', 'a stretch of argumentation' and 'a deduction'; and later in the text (e.g., on p. 16) he uses the term 'derivation'. One should always be able to tell from the context how such terms are being employed, but to avoid any possible confusion I'll use only 'deduction' in referring to arguments of this second kind. The term 'argument' will be reserved for arguments of the first kind.

For Lemmon, then, a <u>deduction</u> is a finite list of propositions each of which is either an <u>assumption</u> (a line derived from no earlier line(s), but merely taken for granted) or a line gotten by applying a <u>rule of derivation</u> to an earlier line or lines. Lines to which a rule of derivation has been applied to obtain a later line (i) are the <u>premisses</u> for (i), and line (i) itself is <u>the conclusion drawn</u> from those premisses. The last line of a deduction is <u>the conclusion of the deduction</u>.

Lemmon sometimes (e.g., on p. 13) calls rules of derivation 'valid' or 'sound'. A rule is <u>sound</u> if it can never lead from true premisses to a false conclusion. This is the kind of rule you'll be studying, and its interest should be obvious: any conclusion drawn from true premisses by means of such a rule must itself be true. Though Lemmon never talks of the "validity" or "soundness" of deductions, it would be natural to say (and many logicians do) that a deduction is <u>sound</u> (or <u>valid</u>) if its every line is either an assumption or a line gotten by applying a sound rule of derivation to an earlier line or lines.

By way of illustration, consider the following deduction annotated in the way Lemmon describes on pp. 8-9:

$(\mathcal{D})$

1	(1)	All women are mortal	A
1	(2)	If Xanthippe is a woman, then Xanthippe is mortal	1 UE

```
3 (3) Xanthippe is a woman          A
1, 3 (4) Xanthippe is mortal        2, 3  MPP
```

The numbers in parentheses serve merely to number the lines, while the 'A' to the right of lines (1) and (3) indicates that these two lines are assumptions. The '1' and 'UE' to the right of line (2) indicate that that line is the conclusion drawn by applying rule UE (a rule you'll encounter in Chapter 3) to line (1); so line (1) is the premiss for line (2). Likewise, line (4) is the conclusion drawn from lines (2) and (3) by rule MPP; so (2) and (3) are the premisses for line (4), the conclusion of the deduction. Since the rules UE and MPP are both sound, the deduction itself is sound.

The numbers to the left of the line numbers indicate the assumptions upon which the line in question rests or depends-- what Lemmon sometimes calls 'the assumptions of the line', 'the assumptions at the line' or 'the assumptions on the left' (e.g., on p. 16).

Unfortunately, Lemmon says precious little about this idea of a line resting upon assumptions, though the notion is of the utmost importance. Intuitively, what's going on is this. A distinction must be drawn between what is expressed at a given line and what has been shown at that point in the deduction. They don't come to the same thing. In the deduction $\mathcal{D}$, for instance, what's expressed at line (4) is that Xanthippe is mortal, but what's been shown is only that if lines (1) and (3) are true, then Xanthippe is mortal. We say accordingly that line (4) rests upon (1) and (3).

The assumptions upon which a given line rests are determined by how that line was introduced into the deduction. They can be thought of as those assumptions it would be relevant to attack if one didn't want to be committed to what's expressed at the line in question, given that the line was obtained in the way it was. The point is, there are only two ways to deny that a deduction establishes the truth of a given line: fault the reasoning

leading to that line, or question the truth of one of the
assumptions from which that reasoning proceeds. Not just any
assumption can be questioned for this purpose; those that can
are the assumptions upon which the line in question rests. In
the special case where the deduction is sound, they are the ones
from which the line has been shown to follow.

In our sample deduction, lines (1) and (3) rest upon
themselves since they are assumptions it would certainly be
relevant to question if one wanted to deny that D establishes
the truth of those lines. (All that is shown at a line introduced
by assumption is that if that assumption is true, then that assumption is true. This is why Lemmon's Rule of Assumptions is so
innocuous.) And these are the only assumptions it would be
relevant to question for this purpose. The truth of assumption
(1), for example, is simply irrelevant to whether or not Xanthippe
has been shown to be a woman at line (3).

Now if one wanted to deny that D establishes the truth
of the conditional at line (2), one would have to question the
truth of line (1), from which (2) was validly derived. But the
only assumption it would be relevant to question if one didn't
want to be committed to (1) is (1) itself; so (2) rests upon (1).

Finally, line (4) rests upon (1) and (3) because, given
the way (4) was obtained, the only way one could successfully
argue that D fails to establish at (4) that Xanthippe is mortal
is by showing that it fails to establish the truth of line (2)
or of line (3); and the only assumptions it would be relevant
to attack for that purpose are (1) and (3), the assumptions upon
which (2) and (3) rest. (Line (4) rests upon (1) and (3) because
(2) and (3) rest upon these assumptions, not because these were
all the assumptions used to get to (4). In general, lines of
deductions don't rest upon all the assumptions made up to that
point, nor even upon all the assumptions used to derive those
lines.)

Since you'll be concerned in this text to learn how to
recognize what's been shown at any given point in a deduction,

each rule of derivation you'll be studying comes with instructions for determining what rests upon what. In most cases, the instructions are relatively straightforward. In a few cases, however, such as those of A, CP, vE, RAA and EE, matters may not seem so obvious and you should find it helpful to remember the intuitive account given here. Indeed, with the introduction of each new rule of derivation, you should use this account to convince yourself that the given instructions are the appropriate ones.

ARGUMENTS AND DEDUCTIONS: THE CONNECTION. Now what's the relationship between arguments and deductions? It's by means of the latter that one can establish the soundness of the former, for <u>an argument with premisses</u> P, Q, ... <u>and conclusion</u> R <u>is sound if and only if there exists a sound deduction having</u> R <u>as conclusion resting upon</u> P, Q, ... <u>as assumptions</u>. We say that such a deduction proves (establishes, demonstrates) the soundness of the argument in question. (Thus, e.g., our sample deduction D establishes the soundness of argument A.)

PROOFS. This is only the beginning of the story, however. A mathematician is apt to be less interested in the fact that $2 \times (5 + 3) = (2 \times 5) + (2 \times 3)$ than in the fact that every equation of the form $a \times (b + c) = (a \times b) + (a \times c)$ is true. Likewise, the primary concern of logicians is not with showing the soundness of this or that particular argument, but with showing that <u>all</u> arguments of a certain <u>form</u> are sound. (This concern with generality is in fact one of the things that makes both mathematics and logic sciences rather than mere crafts.

To this end, logicians construct <u>formal languages</u> whose sentences (or <u>wffs</u>) express (exhibit, represent) the <u>logical forms</u> of propositions. (Thus, e.g., Lemmon uses the expression '$(P \rightarrow -Q)$' as a wff expressing the logical form of any conditional proposition whose consequent is a negation. Here, as in general, the <u>grammatical</u> form of the wff mirrors part of the logical form expressed by it.) Now, as it happens, the soundness of an

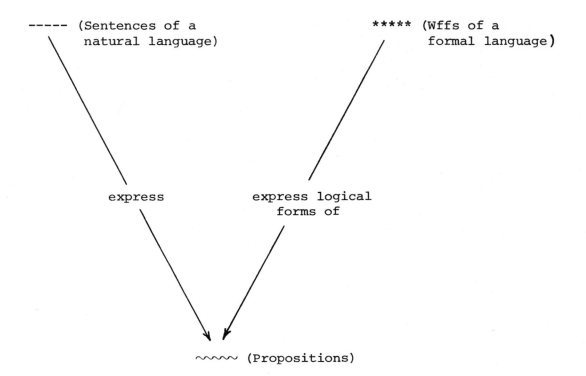

FIGURE 1

argument is a function solely of the logical forms of its con-
stituent propositions. Since the logician is concerned only with
the soundness of arguments, these "wffs" therefore exhibit the
only feature of propositions in which he has any real interest
--viz., a certain <u>structure</u>. But this means that instead of
studying propositions directly, he could just as well study
the <u>wffs themselves</u>, much as a chemist might study plastic
molecular models rather than actual molecules. And this is
precisely what the logician does. In so doing, of course, he
is still studying the logical behavior of propositions, just as
the chemist, in playing with his models, is learning about real
molecules. He's just going about it indirectly, exploiting the
fact that wffs and propositions are structurally **similar.**

   The advantage of this roundabout approach is that the
study of logic is now focused on the <u>forms</u> of sound arguments,
thereby lending the subject the desired degree of generality.
There's a second advantage as well: wffs are easier to study
than actual propositions, being simple linguistic items (things
that can be written down and inspected) rather than abstract
entities which somehow lurk behind declarative sentences. (If
the logical forms of propositions always **coincided** with the
grammatical forms of the sentences which express them, things
wouldn't be so bad. But notoriously they don't.)
   What you'll be studying, then, at least directly, are
not actual deductions, but what (on p. 11) Lemmon calls 'proofs'.
A <u>proof</u> is a finite list of wffs each of which is either an
<u>assumption</u> (a line introduced by rule A) or a line gotten by
applying a rule of derivation to an earlier line or lines. As
with deductions, lines of proofs to which a rule of derivation
has been applied to obtain a later line (i) are the <u>premisses</u>
for (i), and line (i) itself is <u>the conclusion drawn</u> from those
premisses. The last line of a proof is <u>the conclusion of the
proof</u>. If you like, you can think of proofs as expressing
(exhibiting, representing) the logical forms of deductions.

For example, the following (annotated) proof:

(P)

	1	(1)	$(x)(Wx \rightarrow Mx)$	A
	1	(2)	$Wn \rightarrow Mn$	1 UE
	3	(3)	Wn	A
1,	3	(4)	Mn	2, 3 MPP

expresses the logical form of the deduction D. (The four wffs '$(x)(Wx \rightarrow Mx)$', '$Wn \rightarrow Mn$', 'Wn' and 'Mn' will be explained in Chapters 3 and 4.)

A proof is <u>sound</u> (or <u>valid</u>) if every deduction of the form expressed by the proof is sound. Lines of proofs are said to <u>rest</u> or <u>depend</u> upon assumptions in a sense analogous to that in which lines of deductions rest or depend upon their assumptions.

RULES OF DERIVATION. You may have noticed that the lines of proof P were introduced by the same rules as were the lines of deduction D. But how could this be? The lines of proofs are wffs, while those of deductions are propositions. In citing the same rules in both cases, haven't I just equivocated--first treating UE and MPP as if they were rules applying to propositions, then as rules applying to wffs?

Strictly speaking, I have; and this same equivocation is found throughout Lemmon's text. He actually gives you two versions of each of his rules, but never makes a point of distinguishing them. MTT, for example, when first introduced on p. 12, is stated in the "material mode":

(MTT_1) Given a conditional proposition and the negation of its consequent, one may derive the negation of its antecedent resting upon the same assumptions as the premisses.

On p. 40, however, the rule is stated in the "formal mode":

(MTT$_2$) Given a wff of the form A → B and the
corresponding wff -B, one may derive the
wff -A resting upon the same assumptions
as the premisses.

(The statement of MTT on p. 40 has to be read this way since,
for Lemmon, the letters 'A' and 'B' **stand for**
wffs and not propositions. See p. 49.) The first way of putting
it would be appropriate only if MTT were a rule governing <u>deduc-</u>
<u>tions</u>. Since you'll be constructing <u>proofs</u>, as does Lemmon himself,
MTT$_2$ should be construed as his official version of that rule.
Likewise with each of his rules: it's the "formal mode" version
that you and he are actually using.

Lemmon isn't merely being "sloppy" here. There's a
good pedagogical reason for his equivocation having to do with
the way in which the text is organized. The idea of a formal
language, and of "modelling" propositions with wffs, are ideas
which give many students trouble upon first acquaintance. So
rather than hit you with it all at once, Lemmon has chosen to ease
you into the subject informally in Chapters 1 and 3. By the time
you get around to the more rigorous (official) treatment in Chapters 2 and 4, you'll have already gained a working familiarity,
both with the grammar of the languages of the propositional and
predicate calculi and with his rules of derivation. The price is
a little equivocation. Wffs and proofs are conflated with propositions and deductions, and the "formal mode" versions of Lemmon's
rules are conflated with their "material mode" analogs. Likewise,
terms such as 'conditional', 'negation', 'double negation',
'conjunction' and 'disjunction' sometimes refer to propositions
of certain logical forms, and sometimes to wffs of analogous
grammatical forms. This shouldn't cause any serious confusion,
though, as long as you're aware of what he's doing. Besides,
this casual way of proceeding has the virtue of keeping your
eye on the relevance of the study of proofs to our <u>ultimate</u>
concern: the arguments and deductions with which we all have
to contend in our everyday lives.

Once you realize that proofs are lists of <u>expressions</u>, and that Lemmon's rules of derivation apply to those expressions and not to propositions, some otherwise curious passages in the text become clear.

To take just one example, look at the proof at the top of p. 14. Lemmon cautions that one cannot use MTT on lines (1) and (2) to get line (4), but must first use DN at line (3) and then apply MTT to (1) and (3). But why, if MTT were a rule applying to propositions? If, as Lemmon maintains on p. 13, a proposition and its double negation are identical, then the proposition that Q and the proposition that --Q are one and the same. And this would mean that the negation of the consequent of (1) <u>does</u> appear on line (2), so MTT could be applied to those two lines after all.

The answer, of course, is that by MTT Lemmon has in mind MTT_2, not MTT_1. By the consequent of (1) he means '-Q', and the negation of this is the <u>wff</u> '--Q'--the expression gotten by placing a slash in front of '-Q'. But then the negation of the consequent of (1) appears only at line (3), as Lemmon claims, and not at (2), for 'Q' and '--Q' are not the same <u>expressions</u>. ('Q' and '--Q' may express logical forms of the same propositions, but they are not <u>themselves</u> identical--one consists of three symbols, the other only one.)

SEQUENTS AND SEQUENT-EXPRESSIONS. Finally, what does a proof prove?

Expressions such as

(*SE*) $(x)(Wx \rightarrow Mx)$, Wn $\vdash$ Mn

consisting of a (possibly empty) series of wffs separated by commas, and followed by '$\vdash$' and another wff, are what Lemmon calls 'sequent-expressions' (see p. 48). Sequent-expressions express (exhibit, represent) <u>sequents</u>--'sequent' being Lemmon's technical term for the logical form of an argument (he also uses the phrase 'argument-frame' on p. 12). (Thus, e.g., *SE* expresses

a sequent which is the logical form of argument A.) Lemmon
frequently speaks of sequents where, strictly speaking, he means
sequent-expressions (see, e.g., the first paragraph on p. 12).
Again, this is due primarily to the organization of the text,
as with his conflation of propositions and wffs. And again,
this should be the source of no serious confusion.

A sequent is <u>sound</u> (or <u>valid</u>) if and only if every
argument of that form is sound. And a sequent-expression is
<u>sound</u> (or <u>valid</u>, or 'tautologous' as Lemmon says in Chapter 2)
just in case it expresses a sound sequent. Proofs thus stand to
sequent-expressions as deductions stand to arguments, for <u>a</u>
<u>sequent-expression</u>

$$A_1, \ldots, A_n \vdash B$$

<u>**is sound if and only if there exists a sound proof** having</u>
B <u>as conclusion resting upon</u> $A_1, \ldots, A_n$ <u>as assumptions</u>. Such a
proof <u>proves</u> the sequent-expression in question. (In the footnote
on p. 12, Lemmon remarks that one might also say here that the
proof <u>proves</u> B <u>from</u> $A_1, \ldots, A_n$.)

Lemmon generally speaks of proving sequents, rather than
sequent-expressions, but this is best construed merely as a
shorthand way of saying "prove to be sound (or valid)." It's
the soundness (or validity) of a sequent that one proves, not
the sequent itself. And this is done by proving a sequent-expression
expressing that sequent. (When, in Ex. 1 on p. 18, you're asked
to "find proofs of the following sequents," it's the sequent-
expressions there inscribed that you're to prove. In so doing,
you "prove" the sequents they express. Thus, e.g., in proving
SE one thereby "proves" the sequent expressed by it, i.e.,
proves A to be of a sound logical form.)

The wffs to the left of ' $\vdash$ ' in a sequent-expression are
its <u>assumptions</u> and the wff to the right its <u>conclusion</u>. (E.g.,
'(x)(Wx → Mx)' and 'Wn' are the assumptions of *SE*, while its
conclusion is 'Mn'.) Likewise, the logical forms expressed by

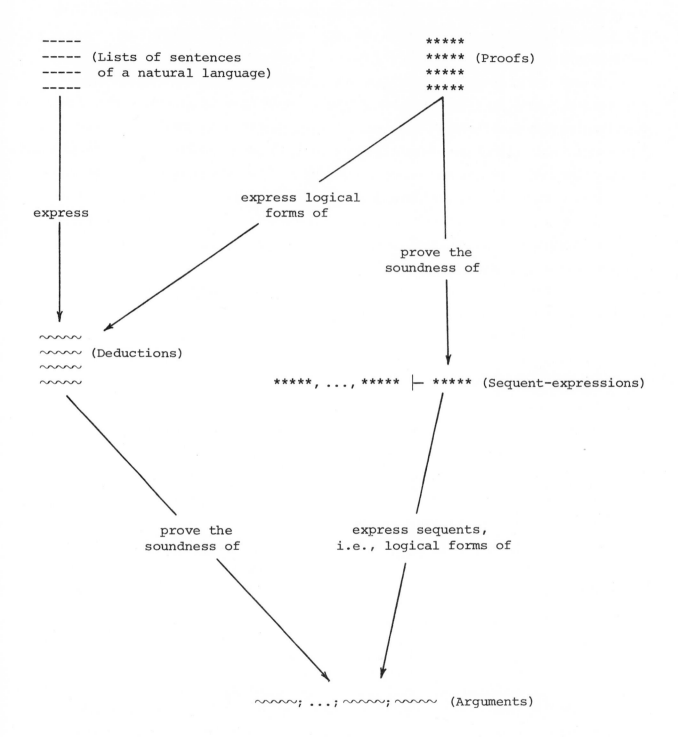

FIGURE 2

the assumptions (conclusion) of a given sequent-expression are
the <u>assumptions</u> (<u>conclusion</u>) of the sequent expressed by that
sequent-expression (see p. 12).

Given the relationship between sequent-expressions and
arguments, and the terminology used in connection with the latter,
one might have expected Lemmon to use 'premiss' here in place of
'assumption'. That he doesn't results from the fact that he actually
thinks of sequent-expressions in two different ways. He views
them both (i) as exhibiting the logical forms of arguments and
(ii) as just a shorthand way of saying "Given as assumptions
propositions of forms..., one can validly derive the corresponding
proposition of the form..." (see p. 11). This ambiguity is relatively harmless, of course, since a sequent-expression will
exhibit a sound argument-form if and only if, from the premisses
of any argument of that form, taken as assumptions, one can
validly derive the conclusion of the argument. Just keep in mind
that Lemmon sometimes thinks of sequent-expressions in one way,
sometimes in the other.

The fact that Lemmon thinks of sequent-expressions in way
(ii) serves also to explain why it is appropriate to talk of
"proving" them. In constructing a proof of a sequent-expression,
you're indeed proving (i.e., proving true) a sentence--a sentence
of the form 'Given as assumptions propositions of such-and-such
forms, one can validly derive the corresponding proposition of
thus-and-such form'. And you're doing this by showing how such
a derivation or deduction would go; you're showing what <u>form</u>
it would have.

* * * * *

In sum, then, the logician adopts the following procedure
for showing an argument to be sound. The sentences expressing the
argument are first translated into wffs of some appropriate
formal language. These wffs are used to form a sequent-expression
exhibiting the logical form of the given argument. Using sound

rules of derivation, a proof is then constructed of this sequent-expression, thereby establishing that __all__ arguments of that form (including the given argument) are sound. (Thus, A might be rendered as SE, and this in turn proven using the proof P. A is therefore a sound argument, as is every argument of the same logical form. Of course, the soundness of A can also be established by direct appeal to deduction D, but that approach can become rather cumbersome when dealing with more complex arguments. More importantly, it doesn't yield nearly as much information as does the alternative approach via P.)

2   Which of the following statements are true? (**Recall definitions on p. 3 above.**)   **Explain your answers.**

   (a) No sound deduction has a false conclusion.

   (b) Every deduction with a true conclusion is sound.

   (c) Every sound deduction contains at least one premiss.

   (d) No sound deduction has all true **premisses** and a **false** conclusion.

   (e) Every sound deduction which contains a false line also contains a false assumption.

   (f) If every assumption of a sound deduction is true, then the conclusion of the deduction must be true.

   (g) If every premiss of a sound deduction is true, then the conclusion of the deduction must be true.

   (h) Some sound deductions have all false assumptions and a true conclusion.

   (i) If every assumption of a sound deduction is true, then every premiss of the deduction must be true.

   (j) If every premiss of a sound deduction is true, then every assumption of the deduction must be true.

3   Show the following arguments to be sound. [Notice here, and in subsequent exercises, the myriad ways in which the presence of conjunctions and conditionals are signaled in English. In some of these arguments, certain premises (or even the conclusions) are only implicit and will need to be gleaned from what's said explicitly.]

(a) You say it didn't rain last night, eh? Well, if it didn't rain, the sidewalks wouldn't be wet. But they're soaked. So looks like it didn't _not_ rain, either!

(b) Olga must have played this year. If she hadn't, we'd have been without a decent goalie. But it says here in the Newsletter that we placed our goalie on the All-League Team, which means she had to be pretty good.

(c) This levy fails and the schools will just have to close. You couldn't even pay the teachers. They aren't going to work for nothing, you know. Would you? No, if the schools are going to stay open, you'll need money at least for salaries.

(d) "Me? I always get what I want. If I can't talk that fool, Arlo P. Frozzlbottom, into a large donation, I'll be a monkey's uncle. I hear he's a real sucker. Say, what'd you say your name was?"
"Frozzlbottom...Arlo P."
"Spare a banana?"

(e) Lousy reporters can't do anything right! Let Claghorn put his foot in it and what do they do? --they get every word. If he's in trouble, it's only because they didn't have the decency to misquote him as usual. A rotten deal if ever I saw one. The Senator's statement wouldn't have

caused him the least embarrassment if he just
hadn't been quoted correctly.

4   Show the following sequents are unsound patterns of argument.

(a) $P \rightarrow Q$, $R \rightarrow Q$ $\vdash$ $P \rightarrow R$

(b) $-P$, Q $\vdash$ $-(P \rightarrow Q)$

(c) $-(P \rightarrow Q)$, $Q \rightarrow R$ $\vdash$ $-(P \rightarrow R)$

Chapter 1, sec. 3

1   Show the following arguments to be sound.

(a) Naive realism leads to physics, and physics,
    if true, shows that naive realism is false.
    Therefore naive realism, if true, is false;
    therefore it is false.

> --Bertrand Russell, An Inquiry into Meaning
>   and Truth

(b) The derivative of f is given by $f'(x) =$
    $3x(x + 2)$. Hence $f'(x) > 0$ if both $x > 0$ and
    $x + 2 > 0$ or if both $x < 0$ and $x + 2 < 0$. Thus,
    $f'(x) > 0$ if $x > 0$ or if $x < -2$.

> --Johnson & Kiokemeister, Calculus with Analytic
>   Geometry

(c) If God were all-good, He would want to create
    a world without evil; while if He were all-powerful,
    He could create such a world. Yet evil exists. Thus
    God cannot be both all-good and omnipotent.

(d) According to Steiglitz's Theorem, the null radical,
    if raised to a power of 2n, would have a harmonic
    kernel. But it doesn't, even though I've raised the
    radical to that power. The crucial Lemma 3 upon

which the theorem depends must therefore be
false.

(e) If there is justice in this life, no after life
is necessary. On the other hand, if there is no
justice in this life, then one has no reason to
believe God is just. However, if one has no reason
to believe that, what reason do we have to think
He'll provide us with an after life? So, either
no after life is needed or else we have no reason
to think God will **provide one.**

> --paraphrased from David Hume, <u>An Inquiry Concerning</u>
> <u>Human Understanding</u>

(f) If you want to explain the coordination that exists
between our mental lives and our bodily lives, and
you find the idea of mind-body interaction problematic, it will hardly do to posit God as the cause
of it--as did Malbranche. For either God is mental,
material, both mental or material, or some third
kind of substance. In the first case, the problem
just rearises when you try to explain how it is that
God--a mental substance--could causally interact with
our bodies: Likewise in the second case, one has to
posit causal interaction between God--now a material
substance--and our minds. In the third case, there's
no trouble accounting for how God interacts both with
minds and with bodies: mental events in God cause our
mental lives, bodily events our bodily lives. Nothing
mysterious about that; but now you have to explain
the coordination evidently required between God's
mental life and His bodily life, which takes us
right back to where we began. Nor will it do to
suppose God is neither mental nor material. Surely,
if you can't understand how mental and material
substances could interact, you're not going to

find it any easier to understand how some
third kind of substance could interact with
both.

2   Show the following sequents are unsound patterns of argument.

(a) -(P & Q) ├─ -P & -Q

(b) P → -Q ├─ -(P v Q)

(c) P v Q, P → R ├─ R

3   It sometimes happens in the course of a proof that A
is obtained resting upon various assumptions, whereas what one
wants (needs) at that point is A resting upon those assumptions
plus an assumption B. Show how one could get A resting upon
this additional assumption.

Chapter 1, sec. 4

1   Reading '↓' as 'neither...nor...', define A ↓ B in terms
of the sentence-forming operators studied in this chapter.

2   'Or', in English, has both an inclusive and an exclusive
sense. When taken in the inclusive sense, a disjunction is true
if at least one disjunct is true; while taken in the exclusive
sense, a disjunction is true if exactly one disjunct is true.
'v' represents the inclusive sense. Letting '#' represent the
exclusive sense, define A # B in terms of the sentence-forming
operators studied in this chapter.

3   Which of the two rules, vI and vE, if either, would remain
a sound rule of derivation if 'v' were read exclusively? If either
fails, how would you suggest altering it?

4   Using Df. ↓ and Df. # in a way parallel to Df. ↔, prove

the following sequents to be sound patterns of argument.

(a) P ↓ Q ⊢ Q ↓ P

(b) P ↓ Q, Q ↓ R ⊢ P ↓ R

(c) P ⊢ -(P ↓ Q)

(d) P ↓ Q, P # R ⊢ R

(e) P # Q ⊢ Q # P

(f) P # Q ⊢ P v Q

(g) P # Q, P ⊢ -Q

(h) P # Q, -P ⊢ Q

5   Show the following sequents are unsound patterns of argument.

(a) -(P ↓ Q) ⊢ P * -Q

(b) P * Q ⊢ P & Q

(c) P ↓ Q ⊢ P * Q

6   Show the following arguments to be sound.

(a) Suppose the President signs it. He'll take a lot
    of heat from the liberals. Too much, I'm afraid.
    He won't risk that kind of heat--not if he wants
    to win in the primary. He'll sign it only if he
    doesn't want to get re-elected.

(b) Fritz won't go to the party unless Emily or Mary
    is there. So only if Mary shows will he attend,
    because you can be certain Emily'll go only if
    Fritz doesn't.

(c) Looks like Anne and Sue won't get to see each
    other. Neither Bill nor Sue can make it; nor can
    Anne and Chuck. A real shame...the only opportunity
    the two had to get together.

(d) Election-year politicking is enough to make one
    cry. Neither the White House nor Congress is going
    to budge on tax reform unless one of them compro-
    mises on energy. And Congress sure isn't going to
    do any compromising--not in an election-year.
    There you have it: the White House gives in on
    energy--and you know what that means, good-by
    energy policy!--or else it'll be yet another
    year with no tax relief.

Chapter 1, sec. 5

1   In case you want more practice in proving sequents to
be sound before moving on, here are three suggestions. (i) Copy
the sequents proven in the text of Chapter 1, close the book
and reprove them. (ii) Skip ahead and do Ex. 2.2.1 and 2.2.5.
(iii) Copy the sequents proven in the text of Chapter 2, close
the book and try to prove them. Some of these will provide a
real challenge, but they can all be done with the resources
you have at this point. Moreover, by trying them now, you
may find yourself in a better position to appreciate the
importance of 'derived' rules--a topic to be taken up in
the next chapter.

Chapter 2, Introduction

1   Lemmon identifies the propositional calculus (PC) with
a language. It would be more natural, however, to think of PC as
a logic or theory of deducibility for that language, and then
to identify such theories with sets of rules of derivation.
PC thus emerges as the theory consisting of the ten rules
studied in Chapter 1. It's a theory designed to tell us which
arguments, among those whose logical forms can be represented
in the language of PC, are logically sound.

The reason for insisting upon this distinction between languages and theories of deducibility is simple. One would like to be able to speak meaningfully of competing theories of deducibility for the same language, just as one would of competing physical or sociological theories for the same physical world or the same social groups. (Disputes over what follows from what can, and sometimes do, arise, and one way to adjudicate the matter is to compare and contrast the respective theories of deducibility to which the disputants subscribe. Here, as anywhere else, that theory which best accounts for one's data-- in this case, the judgements we antecedently make concerning the soundness of arguments--should presumably settle the issue.) This would clearly be impossible if one didn't draw the distinction suggested.

2   In Chapter 2, you learned to work with PC, and in so doing you were studying sound patterns of argument. In the present chapter, Lemmon is going to stand back as it were and treat both PC and the language of PC as themselves objects of theoretical interest. He promises to answer three questions:

   (i) Is there any way in which one can reuse old results
        so as to make the construction of proofs more efficient?

  (ii) Is PC too strong? Can one prove too many sequents
        to be sound--sequents one shouldn't be able to prove
        sound? (because they aren't sound!)

 (iii) Is PC too weak? Are there any sequents one should be
        able to prove sound, but can't?

A slew of other questions come to mind:

  (iv) Can one use PC to shed any light on the concept of
        a logical truth?

(v) Are any of the ten rules <u>redundant</u> in the sense that they could be omitted without loss of deductive power to the resulting theory? If so, how would one show this? And which rules are they?

(vi) In this same connection, how would one show that certain new rules of derivation would not increase the strength of PC if added to it?

(vii) Is there any routine, mechanical procedure for constructing proofs, or is that always going to require imagination? If there is such a <u>proof-procedure</u> for PC, how does it work?

(viii) Is there a <u>decision-procedure</u> for PC--a routine, mechanical procedure for determining which sequents can be proved sound? In particular, is there any systematic way of showing that a given sequent <u>cannot</u> be proven sound?

(ix) You saw in Chapter 1, sec. 4 that a number of sentence-forming operators other than 'not', 'and', 'either...or...' and 'if...then...' can be **represented** in the language of PC. Just how strong <u>is</u> the expressive power of that language?

(x) You were told that '→' is to be read as 'if...then...'. But there are many different conditionals expressible in English, and some of them have very different logics. For example, there sometimes has to be a <u>causal</u> connection between the antecedent of a conditional and its consequent before the conditional would be counted true. Sometimes a <u>logical</u> connection of one sort or another. Sometimes a <u>meaning</u> connection. And sometimes not. What conditional(s) have you been studying? Is there any conditional for which MPP, MTT and CP are all

valid rules of derivation? Only one? Several?
And what justifies representing different senses
of 'if...then...' all with '→', as Lemmon would
apparently have us do?

You should keep these questions in mind as you work through this
chapter. Lemmon addresses himself to all of them at one point or
another, and in each case he provides a full, or partial, answer.
(In connection with (x), see the solution to Chapter 3, sec. 2,
Ex. (e) below.)

Chapter 2, sec. 1

1   Which of the following formulas are wffs? In each case,
show that the formula is a wff (if it is) or explain why it is
not (if it is not).

(a) --------------P

(b) -P → Q

(c) (P & Q & R)

(d) (((P → P) → P) → P)

(e) ((P & -Q) v --R)

(f) (-Q → ((P & -P) v -(-Q & Q)))

(g) (((P → Q) v (R & -Q))

(h) -(-P)

2   Which of the following statements are true? Explain your
answer.

(a) '(A → -A)' is a wff.

(b) If A is a wff, then '(A → -A)' is a wff.

(c) P and Q are propositional variables.

(d) 'P' and 'Q' are propositional variables.

(e) If A is '--P', then -A is a wff.

(f) A is a metalogical variable.

(g) 'A' is a metalogical variable.

Chapter 2, sec. 2

1   Which of the following wffs are substitution-instances
of '((P v -Q) → --Q)'? In each case, show that the wff is a
substitution-instance (if it is) or explain why it is not
(if it isn't).

   (a) (R → --Q)

   (b) (((P → P) v -(P → P)) → --(P → P))

   (c) ((Q v -P) → --P)

   (d) ((-Q v P) → --Q)

   (e) ((P v -Q) → Q)

   (f) ((P v -(-Q & P)) → --Q)

   (g) (((P v -Q) v -(R → Q)) → --(R → Q))

   (h) ((P v -R) → ---R)

2   If A contains 47 symbols and B contains 16, could B be a
substitution-instance of A? A a substitution-instance of B? Why
or why not?

3   Why can't one show that MPP could have been gotten as a
derived rule from the other nine rules of PC in the same way as
Lemmon does for MTT on p. 62?

4   Show the following rules to be derived rules of PC.

   (a) Given -A → -B and B, one may derive A resting upon

the same assumptions as the premisses.

(b) Given a proof of -A from A as assumption, one may derive -A. The conclusion rests upon the same assumptions as -A in its derivation from A (except for A itself).

(c) Given A v B, A → C and B → C, one may derive C resting upon the same assumptions as the premisses.

(d) Given A v B and C v (A → C), together with a proof of C from B as assumption, one may derive C. The conclusion rests upon the same assumptions as do A v B, C v (A → C) and C in its derivation from B (except for B itself).

(e) Given A ↔ -B, one may derive -A ↔ B resting upon the same assumptions as the premiss.

5   Explain why neither CP nor RAA could be obtained as a derived rule from the other eight rules of PC.

Chapter 2, sec. 3

1   Show each of the following arguments to be unsound using a truth-table test.

(a) A: "We can't possibly survive without reinforcements."
B: "Well, at least there's some hope then. If help does arrive, we'll make it."

(b) Only if Ralph were an elf, you say, would he know the secret of Keebler cookies? I don't see that. That's like saying that all Ralph has to do to discover the secret is to turn into an elf.

(c) If Alice passed the exam, I guess poor Bo didn't. I know neither one would pass only if the questions were a lot harder than they were last year. But they weren't; they were a good deal easier.

(d) You can't take Art 121 unless you've taken Art
    120. But, Terry, you have to have already taken
    Art 120 unless, of course, they gave you that
    transfer credit you wanted. So either you got
    the transfer credit or you're eligible to take
    Art 121.

(e) There's no way you're both going to take that
    last drink and avoid a hangover tomorrow morning.
    Only by an act of courage, then, are you going to
    fail to avoid a hangover--because it would take
    such an act to keep you from that last drink.

Chapter 2, sec. 5

1   (i) Show that if -A is a theorem, then A is not contingent.

    (ii) Show that if A and B are contradictories, then A v B
is a theorem.

    (iii) Show that if A and B are contraries and C implies B,
then A ├── -C is provable.

    (iv) Show that if A is tautologous and -B is contingent,
then A → B is not a theorem.

2   Show the following to be theorems of PC using the proof-
procedure described on pp. 88-9.

    (a) P → P

    (b) P → (-P → Q)

    (c) (P → R) v (R → Q)

3   The "completeness" of a theory is a measure of its strength.
In this section, Lemmon proves what might appropriately be termed
the semantical completeness of PC--that one can prove every
tautologous sequent-expression, i.e., every sequent-expression

which, according to the truth-tables, ought to be provable in any adequate theory of deducibility. The following exercises concern three other senses of "completeness" which have been of interest to logicians.

(i) Show that PC is not _negation-complete_--that there is a wff A such that neither A nor -A is a theorem.

(ii) Show that PC is _Hallden-complete_--that if A and B share no propositional variables, then A v B is a theorem only if either A or B is a theorem.

(iii) Using the fact that PC is semantically complete, show that PC is _Post-complete_--that if A is a nontheorem of PC and PC_A is a theory (a) gotten by adding one or more rules to PC and (b) whose theorems include every substitution-instance of A, then _every_ wff is a theorem of PC_A. [HINT: Use the fact (see pp. 72-3) that every nontautologous wff has an inconsistent substitution-instance.]

(iv) Using the fact that PC is Post-complete, show that PC is semantically complete. [HINT: Use the fact that every substitution-instance of a tautologous sequent-expression is a tautologous sequent-expression.]

4   The focus of these first two chapters has been on the use of PC in the study of English arguments. But this material, especially that found in Chapter 2, has other uses as well. One of the more interesting and important is its application to the design of switching and computer circuits. If you'd like to pursue this topic, you could do no better than to consult M. D. Resnik, ELEMENTARY LOGIC (New York, 1970), pp. 106-36.

Chapter 3, sec. 1

1   The language of the predicate calculus is rather more complex than that of PC. You may find it helpful, after reading

this section, to read pp. 138 to the middle of 145 and do Ex. 4.1.1 before returning to Chapter 3. It should also prove helpful to read pp. 145-6 and do Exs. 4.1.2-5 as you are introduced informally to the four quantifier rules in this chapter. (In this connection, see <u>Chapter 4, sec. 1</u>, Ex. 1 below.)

2   Translate the following sentences into the language of the predicate calculus using the notation suggested. (If a given sentence is ambiguous, provide the translation appropriate to each of its possible readings.)

(a) A fiend in need is a fiend indeed. [Use 'F' for '...is a fiend in need', 'I' for '...is a fiend indeed'.]

(b) A rectangle is an equiangular parallelepiped. [Use 'R' for '...is a rectangle', 'E' for '...is equiangular', 'P' for '...is a parallelepiped'.]

(c) A Rolling Stone gathers no grass. [Use 'R' for '...is a Rolling Stone', 'G' for '...gathers no...', 'P' for '...is a piece of grass'.]

(d) A ship arrived in port, though none was expected. [Use 'S' for '...is a ship', 'P' for '...arrived in port', 'E' for '...was expected.]

(e) John covets a stamp in Mary's collection. [Use 'm' for 'John', 'n' for 'Mary', 'W' for '...covets...', 'S' for '...is a stamp', 'C' for '...is in the collection of...'.]

(f) Jos loves a good joke. [Use 'm' for 'Jos', 'L' for '...loves...', 'G' for '...is a good joke'.]

(g) Jos loves good jokes. [Use 'm' for 'Jos', 'L' for '...loves...', 'G' for '...is a good joke'.]

(h) To live is to risk pain. [Use 'L' for '...is alive', 'R' for '...risks pain'.]

(i) An egg is used in every cake. [Use 'E' for '...is an egg', 'U' for '...is used in...', 'C' for '...is a cake'.]

(j) An egg is hiding under Bill's desk. [Use 'm' for 'Bill', 'E' for '...is an egg', 'H' for '...is hiding under', 'D' for '...is the desk of...'.]

(k) The whale is not a fish, but a mammal. [Use 'W' for '...is a whale', 'F' for '...is a fish', 'M' for '...is a mammal'.]

(l) If every system fails, not everyone will get hurt. [Use 'S' for '...is a system', 'F' for '...fails', 'P' for '...is a person', 'G' for '...will get hurt'.]

(m) If any system fails, everyone will get hurt. [Use 'S' for '...is a system', 'F' for '...fails', 'P' for '...is a person', 'G' for '...will get hurt'.]

(n) If each system fails, someone will get hurt. [Use 'S' for '...is a system', 'F' for '...fails', 'P' for '...is a person', 'G' for '...will get hurt'.]

(o) There's a time for all seasons. [Use 'T' for '...is a time for...', 'S' for '...is a season'.]

(p) Each of a car's "extras" adds something to its cost. [Use 'C' for '...is a car', 'E' for '...is an "extra" of...', 'A' for '...adds...to...', 'P' for '...is the price of...'.]

(q) If anyone can climb Mt. Pip, it mustn't be very high. [Use 'm' for 'Mt. Pip', 'P' for '...is a person', 'C' for '...can climb...', 'H' for '...is very high'.]

(r) If anyone can pass, Edna can. [Use 'm' for 'Edna', 'P' for '...is a person', 'C' for '...can pass'.]

(s) All that sparkles is not gold. [Use 'S' for '...sparkles', 'G' for '...is gold'.]

(t) If a bully picks on Fred, he'll have to answer to me. [Use 'm' for 'me', 'n' for 'Fred', 'B' for '...is a bully', 'P' for '...picks on...', 'H' for '...will have to answer to...'.]

(u) If a hiker makes it to the top, Sue'll eat her hat. [Use 'm' for 'Sue', 'H' for '...is a hiker', 'M' for '...makes it to the top', 'E' for '...will eat the hat of...'.]

(v) He who laughs last laughs loudest. [Use 'L' for '...laughs last', 'H' for '...laughs loudest'.]

(w) Optimists say it's half full, pessimists half empty. [Use 'O' for '...is an optimist', 'F' for '...says it's half full', 'P' for '...is a pessimist', 'E' for '...says it's half empty'.]

(x) Every man has his price. [Use 'M' for '...is a man', 'P' for '...is the price of...'.]

(y) Everyone needs a friend sometime. [Use 'P' for '...is a person', 'N' for '...needs a friend at...', 'T' for '...is a time'.]

(z) Some people never get a break. [Use 'P' for '...is a person', 'B' for '...is a break', 'T' for '...is a time', 'G' for '...gets...at...'.]

(A) When it rains, it pours. [Use 'T' for '...is a time', 'R' for 'it rains at...', 'P' for 'it pours at...'.]

(B) One who ventures an opinion without forethought lives to regret it. [Use 'V' for '...ventures...without forethought', 'O' for '...is an opinion', 'L' for '...will live to regret having ventured...without forethought'.]

(C) It's a sad day when one can't walk the streets safely. [Use 'S' for '...is a sad day', 'W' for '...can walk ...safely on...', 'R' for '...is a street', 'D' for '...is a day'.]

(D) It's only a fool who cuts off his nose to spite his face. [Use 'F' for '...is a fool', 'C' for '...cuts off...to spite the face of...', 'N' for '...is the nose of...'.]

(E) Any car but a Chevy can be driven by Doe's parents.
[Use 'm' for 'Doe', 'A' for '...is a car', 'C' for
'...is a Chevy', 'P' for '...is a parent of...',
'D' for '...can be driven by...'.]

(F) Any denial of someone's freedom is a denial of
everyone's. [Use 'P' for '...is a person', 'D' for
'...is a denial of the freedom of...'.]

(G) A fortune means nothing if you don't have your health.
[Use 'F' for '...is a fortune', 'M' for '...means
nothing to...', 'H' for '...is healthy'.]

(H) Our accomplishments never match our dreams, if we
dare to dream at all. [Use 'A' for '...is an accomplish-
ment of...', 'M' for '...matches the dreams of...',
'D' for '...dares to dream'.]

(I) Widows get a break that widowers don't. [Use 'W' for
'...is a widow', 'H' for '...is a widower', 'B' for
'...is a break', 'G' for '...gets...'.]

(J) Those who have never won a race have missed something.
[Use 'R' for '...is a race', 'W' for '...has won...',
'M' for '...has missed...'.]

(K) All runners must report to an official unless they
participated in each of the preceding races. [Use 'R'
for '...is a runner', 'M' for '...must report to an
official', 'E' for '...is a preceding race', 'P' for
'...participated in...'.]

(L) Harold can't do every exercise, but Sid can't do any.
[Use 'm' for 'Harold', 'n' for 'Sid', 'E' for '...is
an exercise', 'D' for '...can do...'.]

(M) Roses grow in my back yard. [Use 'R' for '...is a rose',
'G' for '...grows in my back yard'.]

(N) Muons and pions are subatomic particles, while molecules
are not. [Use 'M' for '...is a muon', 'P' for '...is a

pion', 'S' for '...is a subatomic particle', 'C' for '...is a molecule'.]

(O) Some town is between every point east and every point west only if there is a point east and one west. [Use 'T' for '...is a town', 'B' for '...is between...and...', 'E' for '...is a point east', 'W' for '...is a point west'.]

(P) None but the brave deserve the fair. [Use 'B' for '...is brave', 'D' for '...deserves...', 'F' for '...is fair'.]

(Q) None of Mable's children go out without a hat. [Use 'm' for 'Mable', 'C' for '...is a child of...', 'G' for '...goes out', 'H' for '...wears a hat'.]

(R) Nothing ventured, nothing gained. [Use 'V' for '...is ventured', 'G' for '...is gained'.]

(S) Nothing would've happened if someone hadn't panicked. [Use 'H' for '...happened', 'P' for '...is a person', 'F' for '...panicked'.]

(T) No worker will be promoted as long as Smith or Jones is in charge. [Use 'm' for 'Smith', 'n' for 'Jones', 'W' for '...is a worker', 'P' for '...will be promoted', 'I' for '...is in charge'.]

(U) No one except a politician talks as fast as Ziggy. [Use 'm' for 'Ziggy', 'P' for '...is a person', 'C' for '...is a politician', 'T' for '...talks as fast as...'.]

(V) No one loves he who doesn't love himself. [Use 'P' for '...is a person', 'L' for '...loves...'.]

(W) Scoring well on the exam is not sufficient for landing a job. [Use 'S' for '...scores well on the exam only', 'J' for '...is a job', 'L' for '...lands...'.]

(X) All things noble are as difficult as they are rare.

[Use 'N' for '...is noble', 'D' for '...is as difficult as...is rare'.]

(Y) Even the wisest man cannot answer every question the greatest fool can ask. [Use 'P' for '...is a person', 'C' for '...can answer...', 'Q' for '...is a question', 'G' for '...is a greatest fool, 'A' for '...can ask... of...'.]

(Z) You can fool all of the people some of the time, and some of the people all of the time, but you can't fool all of the people all of the time. [Use 'P' for '... is a person', 'T' for '...is a time', 'F' for '... can fool...at...'.]

3   Charlie Brown: "A prophet is not without honor except in his own country and his own house." Lucy: "What's that supposed to mean?"

     --"Peanuts," Columbus Dispatch, 10/24/76

Answer Lucy's question by translating Brown's remark into the language of the predicate calculus.

Chapter 3, sec. 2

1   Show the following arguments to be sound.

(a) All wars are futile, it seems, unless lost to us. If no wars were futile, then, we'd have to win them all.

(b) "Dotty reads all Christie novels featuring Miss Marple." "Didn't Christie write 'Murder on the Orient Express'?" "Yes; but that's a Poirot, not a Marple, and she doesn't like Poirots. If only it was a Marple, she'd read it."

(c) Everyone may stay only if all doors are locked. There's

nothing I can do about that. If Smedley is allowed
to stay, all doors and windows have to be locked
anyway.

(d) A friend of yours is a friend of mine. So you don't
have any friends, because no friend of mine is a
friend of yours.

(e) Jerry Wurf, President of AFSCME, in his letter
appearing in your July 10 issue makes the assertion
that "public employes are taxpayers like anyone else."
But, how can this be? Abolish taxes and real taxpayers
would find their disposable incomes increased. Abolish
taxes and Mr. Wurf and his other "public employes"
would find that their incomes have disappeared.
Contrary to Mr. Wurf's assertions, "public employes"
are not taxpayers...We taxpayers are on to this fact.

> --"Letters to the Editor," The Wall Street
> Journal, 07/19/78

Chapter 3, sec. 3

1   Show the following arguments to be sound.

(a) It's simply not true that all Irishmen like whiskey.
I confess, though, I've never heard of one who didn't
like to take a nip now and again. Some drinkers just
don't care for that particular "shot-in-the-eye."

(b) Some reasoning beings do not employ generalizations.
Remember, only language users employ generalizations.
Now no animal has a language, yet some do reason.

(c) College students support any policy which makes
universities act as bail bondsmen for students. But,
of course, some such policies are paternalistic.
Therefore college students support some paternalistic
policies.

(d) Well, if you didn't call him 'cat', he wouldn't scratch you when you try to pet him. Noah's a very nice cat, but sensitive. Cats like that scratch only when called a rotten name--like the one you perversely insist on using.

(e) Only if it's right for all similarly circumstanced persons to do X is it right for you to do X. Rejection of this principle is not immoral; it's a refusal to adopt a _morality_ at all. That's what's wrong with Egoism, according to which there are acts it's right for one person to perform, but not another, even though the two are plainly similar in all morally relevant respects.

Chapter 3, sec. 5

1   Show the following arguments to be sound.

(a) Some people like no one, and no one likes someone who doesn't like himself. That means that some people are disliked by everyone.

(b) Philosophers all study ethics. So if some philosophers are logicians, some logicians must study ethics as well.

(c) "Everybody doesn't like something, but nobody doesn't like Sara Lee," the ad says. Well, then, I guess either no one exists or else not everything is a Sara Lee product.

(d) Nonsense! If Lodge could do everything better than Jain, then, because Jain can do at least one thing better than anything he can do, Lodge would have to be able to do something better than himself. That's impossible, even for Lodge.

(e) Since...it necessarily belongs to rulers, for the

subjects' safety to discover the enemy's council,
to keep garrisons, and to have money in continual
readiness; and princes are, by the law of nature,
bound to use their whole endeavour in procurring
the welfare of their subjects: it follows, that
it is not only lawful for them to send out spies,
to maintain soldiers, to build forts, and to
require monies for these purposes; but also not
to do thus is unlawful.

--Thomas Hobbes, De Cive

Chapter 4, sec. 1

1   The following restatements of EI and EE are somewhat easier
to grasp than Lemmon's formulations on p. 145.

(EI*) Let $A(t)$ be a wff containing the term t, v be
a variable not appearing in $A(t)$, and $A(v)$ the
result of replacing at least one occurrence of
t in $A(t)$ by v. Then given $A(t)$, one may derive
$(\exists v)A(v)$ resting upon the same assumptions as
the premisses.

(EE*) Let $A(v)$ be a propositional function in v, e be
an arbitrary name not appearing in $A(v)$, and $A(e)$
the result of replacing all occurrences of v in
$A(v)$ by e. Then given $(\exists v)A(v)$, together with a
proof of C resting upon $A(e)$ as assumption, one
may derive C, provided that e does not appear in
C or in any assumption upon which C rests in its
derivation from $A(e)$ (apart from $A(e)$ itself).
The conclusion rests upon any assumptions upon
which $(\exists v)A(v)$ rests or upon which C rests in
its derivation from $A(e)$ (apart from $A(e)$).

Verify that EI* is indeed just a restatement of EI. That is, verify that any line of a proof justifiable by EI is, as it stands, also justifiable by EI*, and vice versa. Do likewise with EE and EE*.

2   Show the following rules to be derived rules of the predicate calculus. (Here A(v) and B(v) are propositional functions in v and A(e) is the result of replacing all occurrences of v in A(v) by e.)

(a) From (∃v)(A(v) → B(v)), one may derive -(v)(A(v) & -B(v)) resting upon the same assumptions as the premiss.

(b) From (v)(A(v) v B(v)) and (v)-A(v), one may derive (v)B(v) resting upon the same assumptions as the premisses.

(c) From -(∃v)A(v), one may derive (v)(A(e) → A(v)) resting upon the same assumptions as the premiss.

(d) From C → (v)A(v), one may derive (v)(C → A(v)), provided that v does not appear in C. The conclusion rests upon the same assumptions as the premiss.

Chapter 4, sec. 2

1   Find interpretations which show the following sequent-expressions to represent unsound patterns of argument.

(a) (x)(Fx → Gx), (∃x)Fx ⊢ (x)Gx

(b) ⊢ (x)Fx v -(∃x)Fx

(c) (∃x)(Fx v Gx), (∃x)-Fx ⊢ (∃x)Gx

(d) (x)(∃y)Fxy ⊢ (x)(y)Fxy

(e) (x)(∃y)Fxy ⊢ (y)(∃x)Fxy

(f) (x)(Fx → (∃y)Gxy), (∃x)Fx ⊢ (∃x)Gxx

Chapter 4, sec. 3

1   Prove the following sequents are sound patterns of argument.

   (a) $\vdash$ (x)($\exists$y)(x = y)

   (b) ($\exists$x)Fx, ($\exists$x)-Fx $\vdash$ ($\exists$x)($\exists$y)-(x = y)

   (c) (x)(x = a) $\vdash$ (x)(y)(x = y)

   (d) ($\exists$x)-(x = a) $\vdash$ -(x)(y)(x = y)

2   Translate the following sentences into the language of the predicate calculus with identity using the notation suggested.

   (a) At least three dogs are mutts. [Use 'D', 'M'.]

   (b) Three, and only three, cats were found at Barney's. [Use 'a', 'C', 'F'.]

   (c) Nothing exists.

   (d) Everything exists.

   (e) Zeus does not exist. [Use 'a'.]

   (f) Clyde is taller than Sue or Harry, but none of the other players. [Use 'a', 'b', 'c', 'T', 'P'.]

   (g) No one but Samantha would say it like that. [Use 'a', 'P', 'S'.]

   (h) Except for myself, only Randolph was there. [Use 'a', 'b', 'T'.]

   (i) All the cats, save Joychunks and Studmuffin, used the litter box. [Use 'a', 'b', 'C', 'U'.]

   (j) Fido is the smartest dog in town. [Use 'a', 'S', 'D', 'I'.]

   (k) There but for the grace of God go I. [This one may or may not need '=', depending upon how it's read. See what you can do with it.]

3   Show the following arguments to be sound.

(a) Unfortunately, Rolf's the only available player.
But, then, at least someone's available.

(b) Sue deserves better. Afterall, if it hadn't been
for her, only Carol would've made it. As it was,
Bill and Ralph made it also. I just think such
efforts should be recognized more than they are.

(c) Chris is smarter than anyone else in the class,
but she's not smarter than Ms. McCutchen. If Ms.
McCutchen is in the class, she and Chris must be
one and the same.

(d) Being omnipotent, God can presumably do anything.
Now either He can create a stone too heavy for Him
to lift, or He can't. If He can, then there's
something He can't do--lift that stone. If He can't,
then again there's a limitation on His power--His
inability to create such a stone. In either case,
God is not omnipotent. But, by definition, a being
that is not omnipotent is not God. Therefore, God
does not exist.

4   Show the following arguments to be sound using Russell's
theory of definite descriptions.

(a) Look, the President is Commander-in-Chief, as is
the best-known peanut farmer in Georgia. But there's
only one Commander-in-Chief. So, like it or not, the
President is a peanut farmer.

(b) The fellow in the corner is a practical joker. He'll
be good for a laugh. You know those practical jokers
--always good for a laugh.

(c) The barber [well-known to all lovers of puzzles]
who shaved all and only those who did not shave

themselves would have to have shaved himself if
and only if he didn't. Therefore, no such barber
ever existed.

Glimpses Beyond

What is the connection between the formal languages
studied in this text and natural languages such as English?
The question admits of a number of different answers depending
upon one's interests, but one way of viewing the matter is this.
Our concern, ultimately, is with knowing which arguments expressible
in English are sound. To give a complete theory of deducibility
for that language, however, would be an enormous task, one
over which linguists, philosophers of language and logicians
are likely to exercise themselves for many years to come. We
might begin instead with a simple formal language like the
language of PC. This is a perspicuous language, amenable to
rigorous mathematical investigation. Moreover, to the extent
that it can be used to expose structural features upon which
the soundness of certain English arguments turn, a theory of
deducibility for that language will shed light on the inferences
made in English. Once we have a good grip on how things work in
the language of PC, we can then turn to the study of richer
languages, such as that of the predicate calculus or the predicate
calculus with identity, with their additional structural features.
The object, of course, is to work up to a formal language as rich
and interesting as English itself--at which time we'll presumably
have achieved the desired insight and understanding. What the
logician is doing is thus akin to the sort of model-building
that goes on in every branch of science. Certain simplifying
assumptions are made at the outset, mathematical models are
created, and as one's understanding grows these assumptions
and the models erected upon them give way to more realistic
models of the subject at hand--be it the physical world,

social structures, economic systems or, in our case, English
and its logic.

Viewed in these terms, you've now taken but the first
few steps in a large and on-going project. Even so, a knowledge
of the predicate calculus with identity is sufficient to enable
you to evaluate most of the arguments you're apt to run across
in practice. If you've taken your study of logic at all seriously,
you should now be more sensitive to how arguments work and, to
that extent, are better able to deal with the world in which
you live. And for most of you, that's enough. It might be of
some interest, however, to take just a glimpse at where one
might go from here.

It's been assumed throughout that the sentences of our
formal languages have only two possible truth-values--'T' (truth)
and 'F' (falsity). This was done primarily for the sake of simplicity.
But it has sometimes been claimed that the sentences of English
can have other statuses as well--perhaps meaningless or neuter--
and this in turn suggests that one might want to see what happens
if our two-valued truth-tables are replaced by three-, four-,
or even infinitely many-valued tables. Does one get different
logics? And if so, how do they differ? If the issue intrigues
you, you might have a look at N. Rescher, MANY-VALUED LOGIC
(New York, 1969).

It was also assumed that every **term** actually denotes
something and that at least one thing exists in the world, as
reflected in the fact that one can prove as theorems '$(\exists x)(x = t)$'
("t denotes some existing thing") and '$(\exists x)(x = x)$' ("something
exists"). In most contexts, of course, these assumptions are
perfectly harmless: we only infrequently use nondenoting names
and would have no use for the predicate calculus (or anything
else!) if nothing existed. Still, it must be recognized that
English does contain nondenoting names such as 'Zeus', 'Pegasus'
and 'Hamlet' (or will be if one has what Russell called a "robust
sense of reality," for there simply are no Olympian gods, winged
horses or Shakespearian Danish princes amongst the furniture

of the world); and it's certainly not obvious that it should be a <u>logical truth</u> that something exists rather than nothing.

How would our quantifier rules have to change were one to drop these two assumptions? UI and EE could remain as they are, but UE and EI would have to go (and perhaps additional rules adopted). From the fact that every existing thing is a nonfictional entity, for example, one wouldn't want to be able to infer that Hamlet is a nonfictional entity. The problem here with UE is that the universal quantifier, as Lemmon construes it, ranges over all <u>existing</u> things. Thus, from the fact that everything (every existing thing) has a certain property, it simply doesn't follow that the nonexisting Hamlet has that property. Unless the quantifier is reconstrued as ranging over some larger universe of discourse (including perhaps fictional entities, mere <u>possibilia</u>, <u>impossibilia</u>, and their like) or is given a very different semantical treatment than that which Lemmon has in mind, UE will have to be replaced with:

> (UEF) Let A(v) be a propositional function in v
> and A(t) be the result of replacing all occur-
> rences of v in A(v) by t. Then from (v)A(v) <u>and</u>
> (∃v)(v = t), one may derive A(t) resting upon
> the same assumptions as the premisses.

Likewise, one shouldn't be able to infer that winged horses exist from the truth of 'Pegasus is a winged horse'. From the fact that something has φ, it doesn't follow that there exists something with φ--not unless the "something" in question exists. EI should therefore be replaced with something like:

> (EIF) Let A(t) be a wff containing the term t, v be
> a variable not appearing in A(t), and A(v) be
> the result of replacing at least one occurrence
> of t in A(t) by v. Then from A(t) <u>and</u> (∃v)(v = t),

one may derive $(\exists v)A(v)$ resting upon the same assumptions as the premisses.

One might even want to question the rule =I. Some philosophers of language have maintained that every sentence containing a nondenoting name is actually <u>truth-valueless</u>. Assuming that one still wants sound rules of derivation to be truth-preserving (as opposed, say, to merely nonfalsehood-preserving), =I would have to give way on this view to:

(=IF) From $(\exists v)(v = t)$, one may derive $t = t$ resting upon the same assumptions as the premiss.

Theories of deducibility based on these these weaker quantifier and identity rules, known as <u>free logics</u>, have been studies exhaustively in recent years and tie-up with interesting question in metaphysics and the philosophy of language. A good discussion of the topic, together with further literature references, can be found in K. Lambert & B. C. van Fraassen, DERIVATION AND COUNTEREXAMPLE: AN INTRODUCTION TO PHILOSOPHICAL LOGIC (Encino, 1972).

Besides modifying Lemmon's account, one could add to it. You've studied in this text only <u>truth-functional</u> sentence-forming operators, but there also exists a large class of non-truth-functional or <u>modal</u> operators of great interest to linguists and philosophers. These include the so-called <u>subjunctive conditional</u> ('if...were the case...would be the case'), <u>alethic</u> operators ('it is necessary that...', 'it is possible that...'), <u>tense</u> operators ('it is always the case that...', 'it was the case that...', 'it will be the case that...'), <u>epistemic</u> operators ('Smith knows that...', 'Smith believes that...') and <u>deontic</u> operators ('it is obligatory that...', 'it is permissible that...'). The study of these operators could proceed much as it did for the truth-functional ones, only one would now be entering a more controversial (and exciting) area.

Thus, for example, if one wanted to study the logic of
necessity and possibility, we might add to our formal language
a new unary connective '□' to be read 'it is necessary that...'.
'it is possible that...' could then be defined as '-□-'. We'd
also need some new rules of derivation, of course, governing
the use of this new connective. Our list might look something
like this:

(□E) From □A, one may derive A resting upon the same
     assumptions as the premiss.

(RN) From A resting on no assumptions, one may derive
     □A resting upon no assumptions.

(NC) From □A and □(A → B), one may derive □B resting
     upon the same assumptions as the premisses.

(BP) From A, one may derive □-□-A resting upon the
     same assumptions as the premiss.

(□I) From □A, one may derive □□A resting upon the
     same assumptions as the premiss.

The first three seem fairly obvious. □E says only that necessary
truths are truths and RN that logical truths are necessary, while
NC captures the venerated principle that only necessary truths
follow necessarily from necessary truths. BP is less obvious,
perhaps, saying that every truth is necessarily possible. □I
is probably even less obvious and may be a rule about which
you have no clear intuitions at all. In fact, it's a sound
rule on some interesting analyses of the concept of necessity,
and not on others.

   The literature on modal logics is growing very rapidly,
and this might provide a fascinating direction in which to go
if you would like to pursue the study of logic further. For
subjunctive conditionals, you should consult D. Lewis, COUNTER-
FACTUALS (Oxford, 1973), and for alethic modal logics a good

place to start is with G. E. Hughes & M. J. Cresswell, AN
INTRODUCTION TO MODAL LOGIC (London, 1968). For tense logic,
see A. N. Prior, TIME AND MODALITY (Oxford, 1957) and PAST,
PRESENT AND FUTURE (Oxford, 1967); for epistemic logic, J.
Hintikka, KNOWLEDGE AND BELIEF: AN INTRODUCTION TO THE LOGIC OF
THE TWO NOTIONS (Ithaca, 1962); and for deontic logic, DEONTIC
LOGIC: INTRODUCTORY AND SYSTEMATIC READINGS, ed. by R. Hilpinen
(Dordrecht, 1971), especially the essays by D. Føllesdal & R.
Hilpinen and J. Hintikka. Or, for a more elementary treatment
of these topics, see Chapter Ten of R. L. Purtill, LOGIC:
ARGUMENT, REFUTATION, AND PROOF (New York, 1979).

There are many other things one could do as well. What
about _imperatives_ and _questions_? Do they have "logics," and
are they amenable to the same sort of formal treatment as are
declarative sentences? And what about _adverbs_? From the truth
of 'John walks slowly', for example, it follows that John walks,
and our analysis of the logical behavior of adverbs ought to
help explain this fact. But these questions must remain only
questions for now. In the meantime, try your hand at the
following exercises.

1   Prove the following sequents are sound patterns of
argument using □E, RN and NC, together with the rules for PC.

    (a) ⊢ P → -□-P

    (b) □P v □Q ⊢ □(P v Q)

    (c) □(P & Q) ⊣⊢ □P & □Q

    (d) □(P → Q), -□-P ⊢ -□-Q

    (e) ⊢ -□-(P → □P)

    (f) -□-(P v Q) ⊣⊢ -□-P v -□-Q

    (g) -□-(P & Q) ⊢ -□-P & -□-Q

2   Which of the rules □E, RN, NC, BP and □I are sound when
'□' is read 'it is always the case that...'? As 'it is and always

will be the case that...'? As 'it was the case that...'? As 'Smith knows that...'? As 'Smith believes that...'? As 'it is obligatory that...'? Are there any additonal rules governing '□' you would suggest on any of these readings?

II. SOLUTIONS TO SELECTED EXERCISES FROM THE TEXT

Chapter 1, sec. 2

1   (d)

1	(1)	--Q → P	A
2	(2)	-P	A
1, 2	(3)	---Q	1, 2 MTT
1, 2	(4)	-Q	3 DN

    (g)

1	(1)	-P → Q	A
2	(2)	-Q	A
1, 2	(3)	--P	1, 2 MTT
1, 2	(4)	P	3 DN
1	(5)	-Q → P	2, 4 CP

    (j)

1	(1)	P → (Q → R)	A
2	(2)	P → Q	A
3	(3)	P	A
1, 3	(4)	Q → R	1, 3 MPP
2, 3	(5)	Q	2, 3 MPP
1, 2, 3	(6)	R	4, 5 MPP
1, 2	(7)	P → R	3, 6 CP
1	(8)	(P → Q) → (P → R)	2, 7 CP

    (n)

1	(1)	P	A
2	(2)	-(Q → R) → -P	A
3	(3)	-R	A
1	(4)	--P	1 DN
1, 2	(5)	--(Q → R)	2, 4 MTT
1, 2	(6)	Q → R	5 DN

```
        1, 2, 3  (7)  -Q                                   3, 6  MTT
           1, 2  (8)  -R → -Q                              3, 7  CP
              1  (9)  (-(Q → R) → -P) → (-R → -Q)          2, 8  CP
```

Chapter 1, sec. 3

```
1      (c)       1  (1)  (P → Q) & (P → R)        A
                 1  (2)  P → Q                    1 &E
                 1  (3)  P → R                    1 &E
                 4  (4)  P                        A
              1, 4  (5)  Q                        2, 4  MPP
              1, 4  (6)  R                        3, 4  MPP
              1, 4  (7)  Q & R                    5, 6  &I
                 1  (8)  P → (Q & R)              4, 7  CP

       (f)       1  (1)  (P → R) & (Q → R)        A
                 1  (2)  P → R                    1 &E
                 1  (3)  Q → R                    1 &E
                 4  (4)  P v Q                    A
                 5  (5)  P                        A
              1, 5  (6)  R                        2, 5  MPP
                 7  (7)  Q                        A
              1, 7  (8)  R                        3, 7  MPP
              1, 4  (9)  R                        4, 5, 6, 7, 8 vE
                 1 (10)  (P v Q) → R              4, 9  CP

       (j)       1  (1)  -P → P      A
                 2  (2)  -P          A
              1, 2  (3)  P           1, 2  MPP
              1, 2  (4)  P & -P      2, 3  &I
                 1  (5)  --P         2, 4  RAA
                 1  (6)  P           5 DN
```

Chapter 1, sec. 4

```
1      (d)       1  (1)  -P ↔ -Q                              A
```

```
      1 (2)  (-P → -Q) & (-Q → -P)        1 Df. ↔

      1 (3)  -P → -Q                       2 &E

      4 (4)  Q                             A

      4 (5)  --Q                           4 DN

    1,4 (6)  --P                           3,5 MTT

    1,4 (7)  P                             6 DN

      1 (8)  Q → P                         4,7 CP

      1 (9)  -Q → -P                       2 &E

     10 (10) P                             A

     10 (11) --P                           10 DN

   1,10 (12) --Q                           9,11 MTT

   1,10 (13) Q                             12 DN

      1 (14) P → Q                         10,13 CP

      1 (15) (P → Q) & (Q → P)             8,14 &I

      1 (16) P ↔ Q                         15 Df. ↔
```

```
(f)   1 (1)  P ↔ -Q                        A

      2 (2)  Q ↔ -R                        A

      1 (3)  (P → -Q) & (-Q → P)           1 Df. ↔

      2 (4)  (Q → -R) & (-R → Q)           2 Df. ↔

      1 (5)  P → -Q                        3 &E

      6 (6)  P                             A

    1,6 (7)  -Q                            5,6 MPP

      2 (8)  -R → Q                        4 &E

  1,2,6 (9)  --R                           7,8 MTT

  1,2,6 (10) R                             9 DN

    1,2 (11) P → R                         6,10 CP

     12 (12) R                             A

      2 (13) Q → -R                        4 &E

     12 (14) --R                           12 DN

   2,12 (15) -Q                            13,14 MTT

      1 (16) -Q → P                        3 &E

 1,2,12 (17) P                             15,16 MPP

    1,2 (18) R → P                         12,17 CP

    1,2 (19) (P → R) & (R → P)             11,18 &I

    1,2 (20) P ↔ R                         19 Df. ↔
```

2   (b)   1 (1) P * Q   A
                   2 (2) P * R   A
                   1 (3) -P → Q   1 Df. *
                   2 (4) -P → R   2 Df. *
                   5 (5) -P   A
                 1, 5 (6) Q   3, 5 MPP
                 2, 5 (7) R   4, 5 MPP
              1, 2, 5 (8) Q & R   6, 7 &I
                 1, 2 (9) -P → (Q & R)   5, 8 CP
                1, 2 (10) P * (Q & R)   9 Df. *

       (e)   1 (1) -P * R   A
                   2 (2) -Q * R   A
                   3 (3) P v Q   A
                   1 (4) --P → R   1 Df. *
                   2 (5) --Q → R   2 Df. *
                   6 (6) P   A
                   6 (7) --P   6 DN
                 1, 6 (8) R   4, 7 MPP
                   9 (9) Q   A
                  9 (10) --Q   9 DN
                2, 9 (11) R   5, 10 MPP
             1, 2, 3 (12) R   3, 6, 8, 9, 11 vE

Chapter 1, sec. 5

1   (d)   1 (1) P v (Q & R)   A
                   2 (2) P   A
                   2 (3) P v Q   2 vI
                   2 (4) P v R   2 vI
                   2 (5) (P v Q) & (P v R)   3, 4 &I
                   6 (6) Q & R   A
                   6 (7) Q   6 &E
                   6 (8) P v Q   7 vI
                   6 (9) R   6 &E

```
    6 (10)  P v R                          9 vI
    6 (11)  (P v Q) & (P v R)              8, 10  &I
    1 (12)  (P v Q) & (P v R)              1, 2, 5, 6, 11 vE


     1 (1)  (P v Q) & (P v R)              A
     1 (2)  P v Q                          1 &E
     1 (3)  P v R                          1 &E
     4 (4)  P                              A
     4 (5)  P v (Q & R)                    4 vI
     6 (6)  Q                              A
     7 (7)  R                              A
   6, 7 (8)  Q & R                         6, 7  &I
   6, 7 (9)  P v (Q & R)                   8 vI
 1, 6 (10)  P v (Q & R)                    3, 4, 5, 7, 9 vE
     1 (11)  P v (Q & R)                   2, 4, 5, 6, 10 vE
```

(f)
```
     1 (1)  -(P v Q)                       A
     2 (2)  P                              A
     2 (3)  P v Q                          2 vI
   1, 2 (4)  (P v Q) & -(P v Q)            1, 3  &I
     1 (5)  -P                             2, 4  RAA
     6 (6)  Q                              A
     6 (7)  P v Q                          6 vI
   1, 6 (8)  (P v Q) & -(P v Q)            1, 7  &I
     1 (9)  -Q                             6, 8  RAA
    1 (10)  -P & -Q                        5, 9  &I


     1 (1)  -P & -Q                        A
     2 (2)  P v Q                          A
     3 (3)  P                              A
     1 (4)  -P                             1 &E
   1, 3 (5)  P & -P                        3, 4  &I
     3 (6)  -(-P & -Q)                     1, 5  RAA
     7 (7)  Q                              A
```

```
       1  (8)  -Q                                   1 &E
     1, 7  (9)  Q & -Q                              7, 8  &I
       7  (10)  -(-P & -Q)                          1, 9  RAA
       2  (11)  -(-P & -Q)                          2, 3, 6, 7, 10  vE
     1, 2  (12)  (-P & -Q) & -(-P & -Q)             1, 11  &I
       1  (13)  -(P v Q)                            2, 12  RAA
```

Chapter 2, sec. 2

2   (a) 1, (c) 13, (e) 51

```
5     (b)            (1)  Q v -Q                TI(S) 44
                 2  (2)  Q                      A
                 2  (3)  P → Q                  2 SI(S) 50
                 2  (4)  (P → Q) v (Q → R)      3 vI
                 5  (5)  -Q                      A
                 5  (6)  Q → R                  5 SI(S) 51
                 5  (7)  (P → Q) v (Q → R)      6 vI
                    (8)  (P → Q) v (Q → R)      1, 2, 4, 5, 7 vE


      (f)         1  (1)  P v Q       A
                  2  (2)  -P          A
                1, 2  (3)  Q           1, 2  SI 52
                  1  (4)  -P → Q      2, 3  CP


      (i)         1  (1)  P → (Q v R)           A
                  1  (2)  -P v (Q v R)          1 SI(S) Ex. 1.5.1(i)
                  3  (3)  -P                     A
                  3  (4)  P → Q                 3 SI 51
                  3  (5)  (P → Q) v (P → R)     4 vI
                  6  (6)  Q v R                 A
                  7  (7)  Q                     A
```

```
          7 (8)  P → Q                    7 SI(S) 50
          7 (9)  (P → Q) v (P → R)        8 vI
         10 (10) R                        A
         10 (11) P → R                    10 SI(S) 50
         10 (12) (P → Q) v (P → R)        11 vI
          6 (13) (P → Q) v (P → R)        6, 7, 9, 10, 12 vE
          1 (14) (P → Q) v (P → R)        2, 3, 5, 6, 13 vE
```

(1)
```
          1 (1)  -Q                       A
          1 (2)  Q → P                    1 SI(S) 51
          1 (3)  P v Q ↔ P                2 SI Ex. 2.2.3(b)
```

6   (i) Suppose A ⊢ B is provable. Then:

```
          1 (1)  A          A
          1 (2)  B          1 SI
            (3)  A → B      1, 2  CP
```

Hence ⊢ A → B is provable. [The other half of 6(i) is similar.]

7   See the solution to <u>Chapter 2, sec. 2</u>, Ex. 3 of Part I.

<u>Chapter 2, sec. 3</u>

1   (ii) (i) is contingent. '((P → P) & (P → P) → (P → P)) →
((P → P) → (P → P)) & ((P → P) → (P → P))' is tautologous and
'((P → P) & -(P → P) → -(P → P)) → ((P → P) → -(P → P)) &
(-(P → P) → -(P → P))' is inconsistent.

2   Define '→' in terms of '&' and '-' (or in terms of 'v' and
'-') and then use the expressions (a)-(p) given by Lemmon on
pp. 71-2.

5   Suppose A has the value T. Then, if A and B are contraries,
B has the value F and -B has the value T. Hence A implies -B.

Likewise, B implies -A.

If A and B cannot both have the value T, then -A and -B cannot both have the value F. Hence -A and -B are subcontraries if A and B are contraries.

6   (i)

A	a	b	c	d
T	T	T	F	F
F	T	F	T	F

         (a) A → A

         (b) -(A → A)

         (c) A → -A

         (d) -(A → -A)

(ii) 32, 2^{2^n}

Chapter 3, sec. 1

1   (m) $(\exists x)Kxx$

       (p) [This one is ambiguous.]
          There is some poor victim who was gotten by everyone.
          $(\exists x)(y)Kxy$
          Everyone is a killer.
          $(x)(\exists y)Kxy$

       (s) $(\exists x)(Gx \ \& \ (y)(Sy \rightarrow Lxy))$

       (v) [This one is ambiguous.]
          There is at least one individualistic sport which
          Tom likes.
          $(\exists x)(Ix \ \& \ Sx \ \& \ Lmx)$
          Tom likes all individualistic sports.
          $(x)(Ix \ \& \ Sx \rightarrow Lmx)$

(x) [This one is triply ambiguous!]

Some boys like very few things--only fast-moving sports.

(∃x)(Bx & (y)(Lxy → Fy & Sy))

Some boys are such that the only sports they like are fast-moving ones.

(∃x)(Bx & (y)(Sy & Lxy → Fy))

Some boys are such that the only fast-moving things they like are sports.

(∃x)(Bx & (y)(Fy & Lxy → Sy))

Chapter 3, sec. 2

1   (e) (x)(Fx & -Px → Kx), Fm, -Km ⊢ Pm

1	(1)	(x)(Fx & -Px → Kx)	A
2	(2)	Fm	A
3	(3)	-Km	A
1	(4)	Fm & -Pm → Km	1 UE
5	(5)	-Pm	A
2, 5	(6)	Fm & -Pm	2, 5 &I
1, 2, 5	(7)	Km	4, 6 MPP
1, 2, 3, 5	(8)	Km & -Km	3, 7 &I
1, 2, 3	(9)	--Pm	5, 8 RAA
1, 2, 3	(10)	Pm	9 DN

2   (i)(c)

1	(1)	(x)(Fx → Gx)	A
2	(2)	(x)(Hx → -Gx)	A
3	(3)	Fa	A
1	(4)	Fa → Ga	1 UE
2	(5)	Ha → -Ga	2 UE
1, 3	(6)	Ga	3, 4 MPP
1, 3	(7)	--Ga	6 DN
1, 2, 3	(8)	-Ha	5, 7 MTT
1, 2	(9)	Fa → -Ha	3, 8 CP

```
          1, 2 (10) (x)(Fx → -Hx)          9 UI

   (f)       1 (1) (x)(Fx v Gx    Hx)      A
             2 (2) (x)-Hx                   A
             3 (3) Fa                        A
             1 (4) Fa v Ga    Ha           1 UE
             3 (5) Fa v Ga                  3 vI
          1, 3 (6) Ha                       4, 5  MPP
             2 (7) -Ha                      2 UE
       1, 2, 3 (8) Ha & -Ha                 6, 7  &I
          1, 2 (9) -Fa                      3, 8  RAA
         1, 2 (10) (x)-Fx                   9 UI
```

Chapter 3, sec. 3

```
1    (c)       1 (1) (x)(Fx v Gx → Hx)      A
               2 (2) (∃x)-Hx                A
               3 (3) -Ha                    A
               1 (4) Fa v Ga → Ha          1 UE
               5 (5) Fa                      A
               5 (6) Fa v Ga                5 vI
            1, 5 (7) Ha                      5, 6  MPP
         1, 3, 5 (8) Ha & -Ha               3, 7  &I
            1, 3 (9) -Fa                     5, 8  RAA
           1, 3 (10) (∃x)-Fx                9 EI
           1, 2 (11) (∃x)-Fx                2, 3, 10 EE
```

[Notice that EI has to be used at line (10) before EE could be used at line (11); one could not have gotten '-Fa' by EE and then used EI. (Why?)]

```
2    (i)(b)    1 (1) (x)(Hx → Gx)          A
               2 (2) (∃x)(Fx & -Gx)         A
               3 (3) Fa & -Ga               A
               3 (4) Fa                     3 &E
```

```
          3 (5)  -Ga                          3 &E
          1 (6)  Ha → Ga                      1 UE
       1, 3 (7)  -Ha                          5, 6  MTT
       1, 3 (8)  Fa & -Ha                     4, 7  &I
       1, 3 (9)  (∃x)(Fx & -Hx)               8 EI
      1, 2 (10)  (∃x)(Fx & -Hx)               2, 3, 9 EE


(f)       1 (1)  (x)(Gx → -Hx)                A
          2 (2)  (∃x)(Gx & Fx)                A
          3 (3)  Ga & Fa                      A
          1 (4)  Ga → -Ha                     1 UE
          3 (5)  Ga                           3 &E
       1, 3 (6)  -Ha                          4, 5  MPP
          3 (7)  Fa                           3 &E
       1, 3 (8)  Fa & -Ha                     6, 7  &I
       1, 3 (9)  (∃x)(Fx & -Hx)               8 EI
      1, 2 (10)  (∃x)(Fx & -Hx)               2, 3, 9 EE
```

Chapter 3, sec. 4

```
1    (c)      1 (1)   -(x)Fx                      A
              2 (2)   -(∃x)-Fx                    A
              3 (3)   -Fa                         A
              3 (4)   (∃x)-Fx                     3 EI
           2, 3 (5)   (∃x)-Fx & -(∃x)-Fx          2, 4  &I
              2 (6)   --Fa                        3, 5  RAA
              2 (7)   Fa                          6 DN
              2 (8)   (x)Fx                       7 UI
           1, 2 (9)   (x)Fx & -(x)Fx              1, 8  &I
              1 (10)  --(∃x)-Fx                   2, 9  RAA
              1 (11)  (∃x)-Fx                     10 DN

     (d)      1 (1)   (x)-Fx                      A
              2 (2)   (∃x)Fx                      A
              3 (3)   Fa                          A
```

```
           1 (4)  -Fa                          1 UE
        1, 3 (5)  Fa & -Fa                     3, 4  &I
           3 (6)  -(x)-Fx                      1, 5  RAA
           2 (7)  -(x)-Fx                      2, 3, 6 EE
        1, 2 (8)  (x)-Fx & -(x)-Fx             1, 7  &I
           1 (9)  -(∃x)Fx                      2, 8  RAA
```

3   (d)

```
           1 (1)  (x)(P v Fx)                            A
           2 (2)  -(P v (x)Fx)                           A
           3 (3)  P                                      A
           3 (4)  P v (x)Fx                              3 vI
        2, 3 (5)  (P v (x)Fx) & -(P v (x)Fx)             2, 4  &I
           2 (6)  -P                                     3, 5  RAA
           1 (7)  P v Fa                                 1 UE
        1, 2 (8)  Fa                                     6, 7  SI(S) 52
        1, 2 (9)  (x)Fx                                  8 UI
        1, 2 (10) P v (x)Fx                              9 vI
        1, 2 (11) (P v (x)Fx) & -(P v (x)Fx)             2, 10 &I
           1 (12) --(P v (x)Fx)                          2, 11 RAA
           1 (13) P v (x)Fx                              12 DN
```

```
           1 (1)  P v (x)Fx        A
           2 (2)  P                A
           2 (3)  P v Fa           2 vI
           2 (4)  (x)(P v Fx)      3 UI
           5 (5)  (x)Fx            A
           5 (6)  Fa               5 UE
           5 (7)  P v Fa           6 vI
           5 (8)  (x)(P v Fx)      7 UI
           1 (9)  (x)(P v Fx)      1, 2, 4, 5, 8 vE
```

      (f)

```
           1 (1)  (x)Fx → P                      A
           2 (2)  -(∃x)(Fx → P)                  A
           3 (3)  -P                             A
        1, 3 (4)  -(x)Fx                         1, 3 MTT
        1, 3 (5)  (∃x)-Fx                        4 SI Ex. 3.4.1(c)
```

```
        6  (6)  -Fa                                      A
        6  (7)  Fa → P                                   6 SI(S) 51
        6  (8)  (∃x)(Fx → P)                             7 EI
     1, 3  (9)  (∃x)(Fx → P)                             5, 6, 8 EE
  1, 2, 3 (10)  (∃x)(Fx → P) & -(∃x)(Fx → P)             2, 9 &I
     1, 2 (11)  --P                                      3, 10 RAA
     1, 2 (12)  P                                        11 DN
     1, 2 (13)  Fa → P                                   12 SI(S) 50
     1, 2 (14)  (∃x)(Fx → P)                             13 EI
     1, 2 (15)  (∃x)(Fx → P) & -(∃x)(Fx → P)             2, 14 &I
        1 (16)  --(∃x)(Fx → P)                           2, 15 RAA
        1 (17)  (∃x)(Fx → P)                             16 DN


        1  (1)  (∃x)(Fx → P)         A
        2  (2)  (x)Fx                A
        3  (3)  Fa → P               A
        2  (4)  Fa                   2 UE
     2, 3  (5)  P                    2, 3 MPP
     1, 2  (6)  P                    1, 3, 5 EE
        1  (7)  (x)Fx → P            2, 6 CP
```

Chapter 3, sec. 5

```
1      (c)              1  (1)  (∃x)(∃y)(z)Fxyz      A
                        2  (2)  (∃y)(z)Fayz          A
                        3  (3)  (z)Fabz              A
                        3  (4)  Fabc                 3 UE
                        3  (5)  (∃x)Fxbc             4 EI
                        3  (6)  (∃y)(∃x)Fxyc         5 EI
                        2  (7)  (∃y)(∃x)Fxyc         2, 3, 6 EE
                        1  (8)  (∃y)(∃x)Fxyc         1, 2, 7 EE
                        1  (9)  (z)(∃y)(∃x)Fxyz      8 UI
```

[Notice that EI had to be used before EE. (Why?)]

2   (c) (x)(Cx → Hx), (∃x)(Dx & (y)(Hy → -Lxy) |—

(∃x)(Dx & (y)(Cy → -Lxy))

```
        1  (1)  (x)(Cx → Hx)                      A
        2  (2)  (∃x)(Dx & (y)(Hy → -Lxy))         A
        3  (3)  Da & (y)(Hy → -Lay)               A
        3  (4)  (y)(Hy → -Lay)                     3 &E
        3  (5)  Hb → -Lab                          4 UE
        1  (6)  Cb → Hb                            1 UE
        7  (7)  Cb                                 A
      1, 7  (8)  Hb                                6, 7 MPP
   1, 3, 7  (9)  -Lab                              5, 8 MPP
     1, 3 (10)  Cb → -Lab                          7, 9 CP
     1, 3 (11)  (y)(Cy → -Lay)                     10 UI
        3 (12)  Da                                 3 &E
     1, 3 (13)  Da & (y)(Cy → -Lay)                11, 12 &I
     1, 3 (14)  (∃x)(Dx & (y)(Cy → -Lxy))          13 EI
     1, 2 (15)  (∃x)(Dx & (y)(Cy → -Lxy))          2, 3, 14 EE
```

(e) (x)(Wx → Mx), (∃x)(Fx & Wx), (x)(Fx → (∃y)Tyx |—

(∃x)(∃y)(∃z)(Fx & My & Tzx & Tzy)

```
        1  (1)  (x)(Wx → Mx)                       A
        2  (2)  (∃x)(Fx & Wx)                      A
        3  (3)  (x)(Fx → (∃y)Tyx)                  A
        4  (4)  Fa & Wa                            A
        4  (5)  Fa                                 4 &E
        4  (6)  Wa                                 4 &E
        1  (7)  Wa → Ma                            1 UE
      1, 4  (8)  Ma                                6, 7 MPP
        3  (9)  Fa → (∃y)Tya                       3 UE
     3, 4 (10)  (∃y)Tya                            5, 9 MPP
       11 (11)  Tba                                A
     1, 4 (12)  Fa & Ma                            5, 8 &I
  1, 4, 11 (13)  Fa & Ma & Tba                     11, 12 &I
  1, 4, 11 (14)  Fa & Ma & Tba & Tba               12, 13 &I
```

1, 4, 11	(15)	$(\exists z)$ (Fa & Ma & Tza & Tza)	14 EI
1, 3, 4	(16)	$(\exists z)$ (Fa & Ma & Tza & Tza)	10, 11, 15 EE
1, 3, 4	(17)	$(\exists y)(\exists z)$ (Fa & My & Tza & Tzy)	16 EI
1, 3, 4	(18)	$(\exists x)(\exists y)(\exists z)$ (Fx & My & Tzx & Tzy)	17 EI
1, 2, 3	(19)	$(\exists x)(\exists y)(\exists z)$ (Fx & My & Tzx & Tzy)	2, 4, 18 EE

Chapter 4, sec. 1

1   (a) wff, (b) neither, (c) propositional function in y,
(d) wff, (e) propositional function in x, (f) wff, (g) wff, (h)
neither, (i) propositional function in y, (j) propositional
function in u

    Verify these answers.

2   (a) and (b) are incorrect. (Why?)

3   (b), (d) and (f) are incorrect. (Why?)

4   (b) and (d) are incorrect. (Why?)

5   (a)(ii), (b)(ii), (e)(ii) and (f)(ii) are inappropriate.
(Explain why.)

Chapter 4, sec. 2

1   (a) Fm v Hm, (x)(Fx v Hx → -Hxa) $\vdash$ --Hma

    (b) (x)(Fx → (y)Gxy), (x)Fx $\vdash$ (x)(y)Gxy

    (e) $(\exists x)(\exists z)$(Fxz & Gzx $-\vdash$ $(\exists y)(\exists z)$(Fy & Gzy)

    (h) (x)(Fxa v (z)Kzx → (z)Fzx) $\vdash$ (x)(($\exists y$)((Fya v (z)Kzy)
            & (z)(Fxz → Gzy)) → ($\exists y$)((z)Fzx & (z)(Fxz → Gzy)))

2   (e)   1 (1) (x)Fx → (x)Gx   A
               2 (2) -$(\exists x)$(Fx → Gx)   A

```
      2  (3)  (x)-(Fx → Gx)           2 SI(S) Ex. 3.4.1(d)

      2  (4)  -(Fa → Ga)              3 UE

      2  (5)  Fa & -Ga                4 SI(S) Ex. 2.2.5(g)

      2  (6)  Fa                      5 &E

      2  (7)  (x)Fx                   6 UI

   1, 2  (8)  (x)Gx                   1, 7 MPP

   1, 2  (9)  Ga                      8 UE

      2 (10)  -Ga                     5 &E

   1, 2 (11)  Ga & -Ga                9, 10 &I

      1 (12)  --(∃x)(Fx → Gx)         2, 11 RAA

      1 (13)  (∃x)(Fx → Gx)           12 DN
```

[(f) is similar to (e).]


```
3     (d)        1  (1)  -(∃y)((∃x)Fx → Fy)      A

                 1  (2)  (y)-((∃x)Fx → Fy)       1 SI(S) Ex. 3.4.1(d)

                 1  (3)  -((∃x)Fx → Fa)          2 UE

                 1  (4)  (∃x)Fx & -Fa            3 SI(S) Ex. 2.2.5(g)

                 1  (5)  (∃x)Fx                  4 &E

                 1  (6)  -Fa                     4 &E

                 1  (7)  (x)-Fx                  6 UI

                 1  (8)  -(∃x)Fx                 7 SI(S) Ex. 3.4.1(d)

                 1  (9)  (∃x)Fx & -(∃x)Fx        5, 8 &I

                   (10)  --(∃y)((∃x)Fx → Fy)     1, 9 RAA

                   (11)  (∃y)((∃x)Fx → Fy)       10 DN
```


4   (a) Let e be any arbitrary name not appearing in A(v),
C or any assumption listed in β . [How does one know there
is such a term?] Let A(e) be the result of replacing all occurrences
of v in A(v) by e.

```
      (EE)                      .
                               .
                               .
                  α   (i)  -(v)-A(v)
                               .
                               .
                               .
```

```
                    j (j) A(e)                              A
                        .
                        .
                        .
        j, [ β ]   (k) C                                    A
                        .
                        .
                        .

                    m (m) -C                                A
    j, m, [ β ]   (m + 1) C & -C                            k, m &I
       m, [ β ]   (m + 2) -A(e)                             j, m + 1 RAA
       m, [ β ]   (m + 3) (v)-A(v)                          m + 2 UI
m, [ α ], [ β ]   (m + 4) (v)-A(v) & -(v)-A(v)              i, m + 3 &I
   [ α ], [ β ]   (m + 5) --C                               m, m + 4 RAA
   [ α ], [ β ]   (m + 6) C                                 m + 5 DN
```

[Notice that UI can be used at line (m + 3) because of the way
e was picked; and (v)-A(v) is what one gets at that line because
of the way A(e) was defined. (Explain.)]

   (b) Let e be any arbitrary name not appearing in any
assumption listed in the box, and suppose v is a variable not
appearing in A(e). [How does one know there is such a variable?]
Let A(v) be the result of replacing all occurrences of e in
A(e) by v.

```
    (UI)                    .
                            .
                            .
                            .
            [     ]    (i) A(e)
                            .
                            .
                            .
            j (j) (∃v)-A(v)                                 A
      j + 1 (j + 1) -A(e)                                   A
    j, [     ]  (j + 2) A(e) & (∃v)-A(v)                    i, j &I
    j, [     ]  (j + 3) A(e)                                j + 2 &E
j, j + 1, [     ]  (j + 4) A(e) & -A(e)                     j + 1, j + 3 &I
   j + 1, [     ]  (j + 5) -(∃v)-A(v)                       j, j + 4 RAA
    j, [     ]  (j + 6) -(∃v)-A(v)                          j, j + 1, j + 5 EE
```

```
j, ▭     (j + 7)  (∃v)-A(v) & -(∃v)-A(v)     j, j + 6  &I
   ▭     (j + 8)  -(∃v)-A(v)                  j, j + 7  RAA
```

[Notice that EE can be used at line (j + 6) because of the way e was picked. (Explain.)]

Chapter 4, sec. 3

```
1    (c)        1 (1) b = a      A
                2 (2) c = a      A
                  (3) c = c      =I
                2 (4) a = c      2, 3  =E
            1, 2 (5) b = c       1, 4  =E
```

[Why was it necessary to use =I here before =E?]

```
2    (c)  (x)(Dx → a = x v b = x), Ta, Tb ⊢ (x)(Dx → Tx)

                  1 (1) (x)(Dx → a = x v b = x)    A
                  2 (2) Ta                          A
                  3 (3) Tb                          A
                  4 (4) Dc                          A
                  1 (5) Dc → a = c v b = c          1 UE
               1, 4 (6) a = c v b = c               4, 5  MPP
                  7 (7) a = c                        A
               2, 7 (8) Tc                           2, 7  =E
                  9 (9) b = c                        A
               3, 9 (10) Tc                          3, 9  =E
         1, 2, 3, 4 (11) Tc                          6, 7, 8, 9, 10 vE
            1, 2, 3 (12) Dc → Tc                     4, 11  CP
            1, 2, 3 (13) (x)(Dx → Tx)                12 UI
```

[Why was the arbitrary name 'c' used at line (4) instead of, say, 'a'?]

```
5    (a)  (∃x)((y)(Ay ↔ y = x) & Dx), Aa ⊢ Da
```

1	(1)	$(\exists x)((y)(Ay \leftrightarrow y = x) \,\&\, Dx)$	A
2	(2)	Aa	A
3	(3)	$(y)(Ay \leftrightarrow y = b) \,\&\, Db$	A
3	(4)	$(y)(Ay \leftrightarrow y = b)$	3 &E
3	(5)	$Aa \leftrightarrow a = b$	4 UE
2, 3	(6)	$a = b$	2, 5 SI(S) 25
	(7)	$a = a$	=I
2, 3	(8)	$b = a$	6, 7 =E
3	(9)	Db	3 &E
2, 3	(10)	Da	8, 9 =E
1, 2	(11)	Da	1, 3, 10 EE

III. SOLUTIONS TO SELECTED SUPPLIMENTARY EXERCISES

Chapter 1, sec. 2

2   (a) False, (c) False, (e) True, (g) False, (i) True

For (a), (c) and (g) consider any deduction which consists of
a single false assumption. The deduction is sound and contains
no premiss.

For (e) and (i) observe that if every assumption of
a sound deduction is true, then <u>every</u> line will be true. This is
because each line is either an assumption or is gotten from
earlier lines by a sound rule of derivation--a rule which, when
applied to true propositions, yields a true proposition.

3   (b) Use 'P' for 'Olga played this year' and 'Q' for 'We
had a decent goalie'. Then the argument is of the form

$$-P \to -Q, Q \vdash P.$$

Prove this sequent to be sound.

(c) Use 'P' for 'This levy fails', 'Q' for 'The schools
will have to close' and 'R' for 'The teachers are paid'. Then

the argument is of the form

$$P \rightarrow -R, \quad -Q \rightarrow R \vdash P \rightarrow Q.$$

Prove this sequent to be sound.

4   (a) Use 'Napolean was French' for 'P', 'Napolean was European' for 'Q' and 'Napolean was German' for 'R'. Then the two premisses are true, but the conclusion false.

Chapter 1, sec. 3

1   (a) Use 'P' for a conjunction of the tenets of naive realism and 'Q' for a conjunction of the principles of physics. Then the argument is of the form

$$P \rightarrow Q, \quad Q \rightarrow -P \vdash -P.$$

Prove this sequent to be sound.

(b) Use 'P' for 'f'(x) > 0', 'Q' for 'x > 0', 'R' for 'x + 2 > 0', 'S' for 'x < 0 and x + 2 < 0' and 'T' for 'x < -2'. Then the argument can can be construed as being of either of the following forms

$$(Q \mathbin{\&} R) \vee S \rightarrow P, \quad Q \rightarrow R, \quad T \rightarrow S \vdash Q \vee T \rightarrow P$$

$$(Q \mathbin{\&} R \rightarrow P) \mathbin{\&} (S \rightarrow P), \quad Q \rightarrow R, \quad T \rightarrow S \vdash Q \vee T \rightarrow P.$$

Prove both sequents to be sound.

(c) Use 'P' for 'God is all-good', 'Q' for 'God wanted to create a world without evil', 'R' for 'God is all-powerful', 'S' for 'God could create a world without evil' and 'T' for 'God created a world without evil'. Then the argument is of the form

$$P \rightarrow Q, \quad R \rightarrow S, \quad (Q \mathbin{\&} S) \rightarrow T, \quad -T \vdash -(P \mathbin{\&} R).$$

Prove this sequent to be sound.

(f) Use 'P' for 'One finds the idea of mind-body interaction problematic', 'Q' for 'One posits God as the cause', 'F' for 'One has failed to explain sucessfully the coordination between our mental and bodily lives', 'R' for 'God is mental', 'S' for 'God is material', 'T' for 'One is left with essentially the same puzzle as that with which one began' and 'U' for 'One will be left puzzled by the idea of interaction between a third kind of substance and both minds and bodies'. Then the argument is of the form

$$R \lor S \lor (R \mathbin{\&} S) \lor (-R \mathbin{\&} -S), \quad T \to F, \quad R \mathbin{\&} Q \to T,$$
$$S \mathbin{\&} Q \to T, \quad R \mathbin{\&} S \mathbin{\&} Q \to T, \quad -R \mathbin{\&} -S \mathbin{\&} Q \to (P \to U),$$
$$U \to F \vdash P \to (Q \to F)$$

1	(1)	R v S v (R & S) v (-R & -S)	A
2	(2)	T → F	A
3	(3)	R & Q → T	A
4	(4)	S & Q → T	A
5	(5)	R & S & Q → T	A
6	(6)	-R & -S & Q → (P → U)	A
7	(7)	U → F	A
8	(8)	P	A
9	(9)	Q	A
10	(10)	R	A
9, 10	(11)	R & Q	9, 10 &I
3, 9, 10	(12)	T	3, 11 MPP
2, 3, 9, 10	(13)	F	2, 12 MPP
14	(14)	S v (R & S) v (-R & -S)	A
15	(15)	S	A
9, 15	(16)	S & Q	9, 15 &I
4, 9, 15	(17)	T	4, 15 MPP
2, 4, 9, 15	(18)	F	2, 17 MPP
19	(19)	(R & S) v (-R & -S)	A
20	(20)	R & S	A

```
      9, 20   (21)  R & S & Q              9, 20   &I
   5, 9, 20   (22)  T                      5, 21   MPP
2, 5, 9, 20   (23)  F                      2, 22   MPP
         24   (24)  -R & -S                A
      9, 24   (25)  -R & -S & Q            9, 24   &I
   6, 9, 24   (26)  P → U                  6, 25   MPP
6, 8, 9, 24   (27)  U                      8, 26   MPP
6, 7, 8, 9, 24 (28) F                      7, 27   MPP
2, 5,..., 9, 19 (29) F                     19, 20, 23, 24, 28  vE
2, 4,..., 9, 14 (30) F                     14, 15, 18, 19, 29  vE
   1,..., 9   (31)  F                      1, 10, 13, 14, 30  vE
   1,..., 8   (32)  Q → F                  9, 31   CP
   1,..., 7   (33)  P → (Q → F)            8, 32   CP
```

This proof will repay careful study as it nicely illustrates the proper use of vE when disjunctions are embedded within disjunctions.

3   Conjoin A and B by &I, and then derive A from A & B by &E. By way of illustration, consider the following proof:

```
      1   (1)  P                    A
      2   (2)  -P                   A
      3   (3)  -Q                   A
   1, 2   (4)  P & -P               1, 2  &I
1, 2, 3   (5)  (P & -P) & -Q        3, 4  &I
1, 2, 3   (6)  P & -P               5 &E
   1, 2   (7)  --Q                  3, 6  RAA
   1, 2   (8)  Q                    7 DN
```

The desired contradiction is obtained at line (4), but doesn't yet rest upon assumption (3) as needed to get '--Q' by RAA. By inserting line (5), however, one again obtains the contradiction at line (6), but now resting upon that additional assumption.

Chapter 1, sec. 4

1   Df. : A ↓ B = -A & -B

                or

     Df. : A ↓ B = -(A v B)

3   Change vI to read: From A and -B, one may derive A v B
(or B v A) resting upon the same assumptions as the premisses.
vE is okay.

4   (c)   1 (1) P   A
                 2 (2) P ↓ Q   A
                 2 (3) -P & -Q   2 Df. ↓
                 2 (4) -P   3 &E
               1, 2 (5) P & -P   1, 4 &I
                 1 (6) -(P ↓ Q)   2, 5 RAA

     (e)   1 (1) P # Q   A
                 1 (2) (P v Q) & -(P & Q)   1 Df. #
                 1 (3) P v Q   2 &E
                 4 (4) P   A
                 4 (5) Q v P   4 vI
                 6 (6) Q   A
                 6 (7) Q v P   6 vI
                 1 (8) Q v P   3, 4, 5, 6, 7 vE
                 9 (9) Q & P   A
                 9 (10) Q   9 &E
                 9 (11) P   9 &E
                 9 (12) P & Q   10, 11 &I
                 1 (13) -(P & Q)   2 &E
               1, 9 (14) (P & Q) & -(P & Q)   12, 13 &I
                 1 (15) -(Q & P)   9, 14 RAA
                 1 (16) (Q v P) & -(Q & P)   8, 15 &I
                 1 (17) Q # P   16 Df. #

(g)

1	(1)	P # Q	A
2	(2)	P	A
1	(3)	(P v Q) & -(P & Q)	1 Df. #
4	(4)	Q	A
2, 4	(5)	P & Q	2, 4 &I
1	(6)	-(P & Q)	3 &E
1, 2, 4	(7)	(P & Q) & -(P & Q)	5, 6 &I
1, 2	(8)	-Q	4, 7 RAA

5   (b) Use 'Harry pays the fine' for 'P' and 'Harry will go to jail' for 'Q'. Then the premiss may well be true even though the conclusion is false. (Harry might pay the fine and still go to jail--perhaps for another crime. This example nicely points up the mistake of always rendering 'P unless Q' as 'P ↔ -Q', as many students are wont to do. In translating 'unless', it might help to read this operator as 'unless perhaps', which is more suggestive of the correct symbolization '-Q → P'. Of course, people sometimes do use sentences of the form 'P unless Q' when they intend 'P if and only if not Q', and in such cases you'll want to use 'P ↔ -Q'. But unless there is a clear indication that a biconditional is intended, you should assume only the minimum and treat 'P unless Q' as a conditional.)

6   (a) Use 'P' for 'The President signs it', 'Q' for 'The President will take a lot of heat from the liberals', 'R' for 'The President wants to win in the primary' and 'T' for 'The President wants to get re-elected'. Then the argument is of the form

$$P → Q, R → -Q, S → R \vdash P → -S.$$

Prove this sequent to be sound.

   (c) Use 'P' for 'Bill can come', 'Q' for 'Sue can come', 'R' for 'Anne can come', 'S' for 'Chuck can come' and 'T' for 'Anne and Sue get to see each other'. Then the argument is of the form

$$P \downarrow Q, R \downarrow S, T \rightarrow (Q \And R) \vdash -T.$$

Prove this sequent to be sound.

Chapter 2, sec. 1

1   (a) Yes, (b) No, (c) No, (d) Yes, (e) Yes, (f) Yes, (g) No, (h) No (You provide the details.)

2   (a) No, (b) No, (c) No, (d) Yes, (e) Yes, (f) No, (g) Yes (You provide the details.)

Chapter 2, sec. 2

1   (a) No, (b) Yes, (c) Yes, (d) No, (e) No, (f) No, (g) Yes, (h) No (You provide the details.)

3   The provability of sequent 55 without the use of MTT, together with the fact that SI [actually SI(S)] is a derived rule, allows one to do everything without MTT that one could do with it. Thus, instead of proceeding:

$$\boxed{\alpha} \quad \text{(i) } A \rightarrow B$$

$$\boxed{\beta} \quad \text{(j) } -B$$

$$\boxed{\alpha}, \boxed{\beta} \quad \text{(k) } -A \qquad \text{i, j MTT}$$

one could get -A resting upon those same assumptions using SI(S):

.
.
.

$\boxed{\alpha}$, $\boxed{\beta}$ (k) -A   i, j SI(S) 55

This shows that MTT could have been gotten as a derived rule from the other nine rules. But Lemmon's proof (p. 58) that SI(S) is itself a derived rule makes use of the availability of MPP, either as a primitive rule or as a derived rule. Use of SI(S) to show that MPP could have been gotten as a derived rule would therefore beg the question.

Aside from the fact that it's not fully general, Lemmon's method of showing rules to be derived (derivable)--by proving appropriate sequents and then appealing to SI(S)--tends to foster misunderstanding. Students are frequently led (i) to confuse sequents with rules of derivation (they are not the same thing) and (ii) to think that derived rules are somehow "proved" much as sequents or sequent-expressions are (they are not).

To establish that a rule is derived, one needs to show that one can get the effect of that rule using primitive rules alone. This is best done directly. Consider again MPP. What that rule says is that given a situation which looks like this:

.
.
.

$\boxed{\alpha}$ (i) A → B
.
.
.
$\boxed{\beta}$ (j) A

one may write down a new line which looks like this:

.
.
.

$\boxed{\alpha}$, $\boxed{\beta}$ (k) B

To see that such a line could be gotten <u>without</u> use of MPP, and hence that MPP needn't have been taken as a primitive rule of PC, it suffices to observe that one could also get B resting upon the same assumptions in the following way:

.
.
.

			(k)	-B	A
k,	$\boxed{\alpha}$		(k + 1)	-A	i, k MTT
k,	$\boxed{\alpha}$,	$\boxed{\beta}$	(k + 2)	A & -A	j, k + 1 &I
	$\boxed{\alpha}$,	$\boxed{\beta}$	(k + 3)	--B	k, k + 2 RAA
	$\boxed{\alpha}$,	$\boxed{\beta}$	(k + 4)	B	k + 3 DN

[Note that line (k + 3) will rest upon everything listed in $\boxed{\alpha}$ and $\boxed{\beta}$, since only assumption (k) is discharged and (k) cannot appear in either of those lists. (Why?)]

More generally, a rule of derivation is a rule of the form 'Given such-and-such a situation, one may write down thus-and-such a line resting upon thus-and-so assumptions'. The most direct way of showing that such a rule is derived, then, would be to suppose that one had such-and-such a situation and then show how, using primitive rules alone, one could get to thus-and-such a line resting upon the appropriate assumptions. This method of proceeding is perfectly general and it serves to underscore what it is for a rule to <u>be</u> a derived rule.

It should not be thought, incidentally, that both MTT and MPP can be eliminated from PC without loss. Each can be, provided that one retains the other as a primitive rule, but nothing here or in the text shows that one could drop the two <u>together</u>.

4   (d)
.
.
.

| | | |
| $\boxed{\alpha}$ | (i) | A v B |

.
.
.

$\boxed{\beta}$ (j) C v (A → C)

      ·
      ·
      ·

k   (k) B   A

      ·
      ·
      ·

k, $\boxed{\rho}$ (m) C

      ·
      ·
      ·

n   (n) A   A

n + 1   (n + 1) C   A

n + 2   (n + 2) A → C   A

n, n + 2   (n + 3) C   n, n + 2   MPP

n + 2, $\boxed{\alpha}$, $\boxed{\rho}$ (n + 4) C   i, k, m, n, n + 3   vE

$\boxed{\alpha}$, $\boxed{\beta}$, $\boxed{\rho}$ (n + 5) C   j, n + 1, n + 1, n + 2,
                                           n + 4   vE

(e)

      ·
      ·
      ·

□   (i) A ↔ -B

      ·
      ·
      ·

□   (j) (A → -B) & (-B → A)   i Df. ↔

□   (j + 1) A → -B   j &E

□   (j + 2) -B → A   j &E

j + 3   (j + 3) -A   A

j + 3, □   (j + 4) --B   j + 2, j + 3   MTT

j + 3, □   (j + 5) B   j + 4   DN

□   (j + 6) -A → B   j + 3, j + 5   CP

j + 7   (j + 7) B   A

j + 7   (j + 8) --B   j + 7   DN

j + 7, □   (j + 9) -A   j + 1, j + 8   MTT

□   (j + 10) B → -A   j + 7, j + 9   CP

□   (j + 11) (-A → B) & (B → -A)   j + 6, j + 10   &I

□   (j + 12) -A ↔ B   j + 11 Df. ↔

5   Any proof employing only the other eight rules will have
a conclusion resting upon at least one assumption. (Why?) But
some proofs using in addition CP or RAA (e.g., the proofs of
the sequent-expressions '⊢ P → P' and '⊢ -(P & -P)') have
conclusions resting upon no assumptions, so neither of these
two rules can be gotten as derived rules from the other eight.

Chapter 2, sec. 3

1   CAUTION: One has to be a little careful when using
truth-tables to show that a given argument is <u>not</u> sound, since
not every argument of the form exhibited by a nontautologous
sequent-expression need be unsound. (E.g., 'P ⊢ Q' is not
tautologous, but there certainly exist sound arguments with
just one premiss!) The sequent-expression used to symbolize
the argument may simply fail to reveal <u>enough</u> of its logical
form--either because one hasn't used all the resources available
in one's formal language or because the needed resources aren't
available. And it may be on those hidden features that the
soundness of the argument turns. (See Chapter 3, sec. 1 for
further discussion of this point.)

    The soundness of each argument in this exercise hinges
solely on its <u>propositional</u> structure--structure that can be
revealed completely using the language of the propositional
calculus. In these cases, then, truth-table tests will work,
provided you expose all of the structure you can.

    (d) Use 'P' for 'You can take Art 121', 'Q' for 'You've
taken Art 120' and 'R' for 'You got the transfer credit you
wanted'. Then the argument is of the form

$$-Q → -P, -R → Q ⊢ R \text{ v } P.$$

But this sequent-expression is not tautologous, since in line
6 of its truth-table both assumptions get assigned T though the
conclusion gets assigned F.

```
P  Q  R  |  - Q → - P, - R → Q  ⊢  R v P

T  T  T  |  F T T F T   F T T T     T T T
T  T  F  |  F T T F T   T F T T     F T T
T  F  T  |  T F F F T   F T T F     T T T
T  F  F  |  T F F F T   T F F F     F T T
F  T  T  |  F T T T F   F T T T     T T F
F  T  F  |  F T T T F   T F T T     F F F
F  F  T  |  T F T T F   F T T F     T T F
F  F  F  |  T F T T F   T F F F     F F F
```

Chapter 2, sec. 5

1   (iii) Suppose A gets T under a given truth-value assignment. Then, since A and B are contraries, B must get F. But if C implies B, then C is given F and -C gets T. So every truth-value assignment under which A gets T is one under which -C gets T, which is to say that A ⊢ -C is a tautologous sequent-expression. Hence, by the completeness of PC, A ⊢ -C is provable.

2   (c) Let B = '(P → R) v (R → Q)'. Then:

```
         (1) P v -P      TI 44
         (2) Q v -Q      TI(S) 44
         (3) R v -R      TI(S) 44
      4  (4) P           A
      5  (5) -P          A
      6  (6) Q           A
      7  (7) -Q          A
      8  (8) R           A
      9  (9) -R          A
 4,6,8 (10) B            4,6,8 SI [use 'P, Q, R ⊢ B']
 4,6,9 (11) B            4,6,9 SI [use 'P, Q, -R ⊢ B']
 4,7,8 (12) B            4,7,8 SI [use 'P, -Q, R ⊢ B']
 4,7,9 (13) B            4,7,9 SI [use 'P, -Q, -R ⊢ B']
```

5, 6, 8	(14) B	5, 6, 8 SI [use '-P, Q, R ⊢ B']
5, 6, 9	(15) B	5, 6, 9 SI [use '-P, Q, -R ⊢ B']
5, 7, 8	(16) B	5, 7, 8 SI [use '-P, -Q, R ⊢ B']
5, 7, 9	(17) B	5, 7, 9 SI [use '-P, -Q, -R ⊢ B']
6, 8	(18) B	1, 4, 5, 10, 14 vE
6, 9	(19) B	1, 4, 5, 11, 15 vE
7, 8	(20) B	1, 4, 5, 12, 16 vE
7, 9	(21) B	1, 4, 5, 13, 17 vE
8	(22) B	2, 6, 7, 18, 20 vE
9	(23) B	2, 6, 7, 19, 21 vE
	(24) B	3, 8, 9, 22, 23 vE

3   (ii) Suppose neither A nor B is a theorem. Then neither
is tautologous. (Why?) So there are truth-value assignments A
and A' under which A and B get assigned F. Let A'' be any truth-
value assignment which gives the same truth-values to the variables
in A as does A and the same truth-values to the variables in B
as does A'. (Such assignments exist since A and B share no
variables.) Since the truth-value of a wff is a function solely
of the truth-values of its variables, A and B will get assigned
the same truth-values under A'' as they got under A and A'. But
then A v B will get assigned F under A''. It follows that A v B
is not tautologous, and so is not a theorem. (Why?)

(iii) Let A be any nontheorem of PC. Since PC is semantically
complete, A is nontautologous. By the HINT, A has an inconsistent
substitution-instance B. Hence, by (b), B is a theorem of PC_A.
But now -B is tautologous and thus a theorem of PC. Hence B
is also a theorem of PC_A, since by (a) every theorem of PC is
a theorem of PC_A. It follows that every wff C is a theorem of PC_A,
for we can construct the following proof:

(1)	B	TI
(2)	-B	TI
(3)	C	1, 2 SI(S) Ex. 2.2.5(e)

So PC_A is Post-complete.

(iv) Suppose PC is not semantically complete. Then there exists a tautologous sequent-expression $A_1, \ldots, A_n \vdash B$ which is not provable. Thus $A = A_1 \rightarrow (\ldots(A_n \rightarrow B)\ldots)$ is a tautologous nontheorem of PC. Now consider the theory PC_A gotten by adding to PC the rule:

(R) One may derive any substitution-instance
of A resting upon no assumptions.

The theorems of PC_A include every substitution-instance of A. However, by the HINT, we know that R introduces into proofs only lines corresponding to tautologous sequent-expressions. Lemmon's proof of the consistency of PC (pp. 75-80) can thus be extended to show the consistency of PC_A. But then not every wff is a theorem of PC_A, which means that PC is not Post-complete.

Chapter 3, sec. 1

2   (b) [This is pretty clearly a _definition_ of 'rectangle' and as such offers _both_ necessary and sufficient conditions for something's being rectangular. Compare with (a) and (c).]

(x)(Rx ↔ Ex & Px)

(e) [Compare with (f), in which 'a' is almost certainly meant to signal the presence of a universal rather than an existential quantifier.]

(∃x)(Sx & Cxn & Wmx)

(h) (x)(Lx → Rx)

(k) (x)(Wx → -Fx & Mx)

(n) [Compare with (l) and (m).]

    (x)(Sx → Fx) → (∃x)(Px & Gx)

(q) [Compare with (r), in which 'anyone' is almost
certainly meant to signal the presence of an existential rather
than a universal quantifier.]

    (x)(Px → Cxm) → -Hm

(t) [Compare with (u), in which 'a' signals the presence
of an existential rather than a universal quantifier.]

    (x)(Bx & Pxn → Axm)

(w) (x)((Ox → Fx) & (Px → Ex))

           or

    (x)(Ox → Fx) & (x)(Px → Ex)

(z) (∃x)(Px & (y)(z)(By & Tz → -Gxyz))

           or

    (∃x)(Px & -(∃y)(∃z)(By & Tz & Gxyz))

(C) [This is multiply ambiguous. About the best that
can be done, given the resources of the language of the predicate
calculus, is to paraphrase (C) in one of the following four
ways--although it's not clear that any one of them fully
captures the intent of the sentence.]

    It's a sad day when there's <u>someone</u> who can't
walk <u>some</u> street safely.
    (x)(Dx & (∃y)(∃z)(Rz & -Wyzx) → Sx)
    It's a sad day when there's <u>someone</u> who can't
walk <u>any</u> street safely.
    (x)(Dx & (∃y)(z)(Rz → -Wyzx) → Sx)
    It's a sad day when <u>no one</u> can walk <u>every</u>
street safely.

(x)(Dx & (y)(∃z)(Rz & -Wyzx) → Sx)

It's a sad day when <u>no one</u> can walk <u>any</u> street safely.

(x)(Dx & (y)(z)(Rz → -Wyzx) → Sx)

(F) (x)((∃y)(Py & Dxy) → (y)(Py → Dxy))

(I) (∃x)(Bx & (y)(z)(Wy & Hz → Gyx & -Gzx))

or

(∃x)(Bx & (y)(Wy → Gyx) & (y)(Hy → -Gyx))

(L) (∃x)(Ex & -Dmx) & (x)(Ex → -Dnx)

or

-(x)(Ex → Dmx) & (x)(Ex → -Dnx)

or

(∃x)(Ex & -Dmx) & -(∃x)(Ex & Dnx)

or

-(x)(Ex → Dmx) & -(∃x)(Ex & Dnx)

(M) [Compare with (N), in which the plural signals the presence of a universal rather than an existential quantifier.]

(∃x)(Rx & Gx)

(P) (x)(y)(Fy & Dxy → Bx)

(T) (x)(y)(Wx & (Im v In) → -Px)

(W) [This one is ambiguous, having at least two readings. The best that can be done, using the suggested notation, is to paraphrase (W) in one of the following ways. To capture the full intent of the sentence, however, one would probably have to use a conditional stronger than the material conditional.]

Not everyone who only scores well on the

exam lands a job.

-(x)(Sx → (∃y)(Jy & Lxy))

No one who only scores well on the exam lands
a job.

(x)(Sx → -(∃y)(Jy & Lxy))

(Y) [What (Y) says is that <u>no one</u> can answer every question
a greatest fool can ask. The reference to wisest men is just
for emphasis, as signaled by the presence of 'even'.]

(x)(y)(Gx & Py → (∃z)(Qz & Axzy & -Cyz))

(Z) (x)(Px → (∃y)(∃z)(Py & Tz & Fyxz)) &

(∃x)(Px & (y)(Ty → (∃z)(Pz & Fzxy))) &

-(x)(y)(Px & Ty → (∃z)(Pz & Fzxy))

Chapter 3, sec. 2

1   (e) This is a very interesting argument from a logical
point of view, one which will repay careful study.

Using 'Q' for 'Taxes are abolished', 'R' for '...is a
real taxpayer', 'P' for '...is a public employe' and 'I' for
'the disposable income of...increases', it's tempting to
suppose that the argument is of the form

(*S1*)   Q → (x)(Rx → Ix), Q → (x)(Px → -Ix) ⊢ (x)(Px → -Rx).

The conclusion is correctly represented; but from the two
assumptions of this sequent-expression one can derive only
'Q → (x)(Px → -Rx)', and not '(x)(Px → -Rx)'. So if the
argument is indeed sound, as intuitively it is, it cannot
be of the form *S1*.

Alternatively, one might take the second premiss of
the argument ("Abolish taxes and Mr. Wurf...") to be the <u>denial</u>
of a certain conditional, in which case the negation would have
large rather than small "scope" as it did in *S1*. On this

reading, the argument is of the form

(S2)   (x)(Rx & Q → Ix), (x)-(Px & Q → Ix) ⊢ (x)(Px → -Rx).

And <u>this</u> sequent-expression is provable. (Prove it.)

   That's not the end of the story, though. One can also prove the following sequent-expression:

(S3)   (x)-(Px & Q → Ix) ⊢ (x)-Ix.

But the second premiss of the English argument hardly implies that <u>no one's</u> income will increase, as the provability of S3 would have it. What this shows is that our rendering of the second premiss is <u>too strong</u>; on the present reading, that premiss implies more than its author surely intended. The provability of S2 thus does <u>not</u> establish the soundness of the argument.

   The immediate source of the problem is the use of the material conditional: the provability of S3 hinges crucially on the peculiar truth-conditions of '→'. But the problem goes deeper than that. Observing that both premisses of the English argument involve <u>subjunctive</u> conditionals (signaled by 'If... were the case...would be the case' constructions), one might think that all we have to do is add to the language of the predicate calculus a new two-place connective '>' to represent such conditionals. We could then take the argument to be of the form

(S4)   (x)(Rx & Q > Ix), (x)-(Px & Q > Ix) ⊢ (x)(Px → -Rx).

Given the very different truth-conditions enjoyed by '→' (and hence the different rules governing its use), the analog of S3, viz.,

      (x)-(Px & Q > Ix) ⊢ (x)-Ix,

isn't provable using any plausible logic of subjunctive

conditionals. Trouble is, neither is *S4!* And this suggests
that there was something wrong with our construing the argument
as being of the form *S2*--something other than just the use
of '→'.

In fact, we picked the wrong predicates. Using 'D' for
'the disposable income of...would increase were taxes to be
abolished', the argument is actually of the form

$$(x)(Rx \rightarrow Dx), \quad (x)(Px \rightarrow -Dx) \;\vdash\; (x)(Px \rightarrow -Rx).$$

Or, if '>' were added to the language of the predicate calculus:

$$(x)(Rx \rightarrow (Q > Ix)), \quad (x)(Px \rightarrow -(Q > Ix)) \;\vdash\;$$
$$(x)(Px \rightarrow -Rx).$$

Both of these sequent-expressions are provable using only the
rules of the predicate calculus. (Verify.)

Two words of caution:

(1) For the purpose of establishing its soundness,
one couldn't construe the argument as being of the form

$$(S5) \quad (x)(Rx \rightarrow (Q \rightarrow Ix)), \quad (x)(Px \rightarrow -(Q \rightarrow Ix)) \;\vdash\;$$
$$(x)(Px \rightarrow -Rx).$$

S5 is provable, but our rendering of the second premiss of
the argument is again too strong (and again because of the
peculiar truth-conditions of '→'). From the second assumption
of this sequent-expression one can derive '$(\exists x)Px \rightarrow Q$'. (Verify.)
And surely the Journal's correspondant didn't mean to imply
that taxes will be abolished if there exist any public
employes!

(2) The problems here generated by the use of '→'
shouldn't leave one overly suspicious of the material conditional, or make one doubt its usefulness in the analysis of
English arguments.

Why study the material conditional if it has the peculiar truth-conditions that it does? Several reasons.

In the first place, they aren't as peculiar as they're sometimes made out to be. It's only when '→' is (mis)read as 'implies' or 'entails' that results like the "paradoxes" of material "implication" (p. 60) seem so troublesome. When 'If ...then...' is carefully distinguished from the very strong relations of implication and entailment, it's not at all clear that the material conditional differs all that radically from the conditionals we find expressed in English. Afterall, 'P → Q' is logically equivalent to '-P v Q', and those circumstances in which we would assent to a disjunction of the form 'Either not-P or Q' are precisely those circumstances in which we would ordinarily assent to the corresponding conditional 'If P then Q'. (Well, aren't they?)

In the second place, assuming that every proposition is either true or false, the material conditional is demonstrably the one and only conditional which satisfies the rule CP. This means that if the doctrine of bivalence--that every proposition is true or false--is correct, then like it or not, every time you use CP either you're making a logical mistake or else you're asserting a material conditional.

Quite apart from whether we ever actually use the material conditional, for many dialectical purposes, both in science and in everyday life, the material conditional is the only conditional needed. Many of the purposes for which we engage in 'if'-y talk can be achieved using that conditional. Indeed, the language of the predicate calculus was originally devised precisely for the purpose of satisfying the needs of mathematical discourse.

Even more relevant, from our standpoint, is the fact that in most cases it's perfectly alright to represent conditionals using '→' whether or not they're material. This point is of the utmost importance, but Lemmon, like a great many

other textbook authors, botches the explanation. On p. 60 one
is told that "...we may continue safely to adopt 'P → Q' as a
rendering of 'if P then Q' <u>serviceable for reasoning purposes</u>,
since...our rules at least have the property that they will
never lead us from true assumptions to a false conclusion,"
i.e., are sound. Now surely Lemmon wouldn't take the soundness
of his rules as showing that, for reasoning purposes, one could
safely render 'P or Q' as 'P → Q'. Why, then, does he think it
shows that one can safely represent <u>nonmaterial</u> conditionals
using '→'?

The plain fact is that indiscriminate use of '→' <u>can</u>
lead to trouble, if one isn't careful. For example, from the
provability of

(S)   P → Q ⊢ R & P → Q

one mustn't conclude that

(A)   If I were to strike this match, it would
          light; therefore, if I were to stand on the
          bottom of Lake Michigan and strike this
          match, it would light.

is a sound argument. For it clearly isn't.

So in precisely what sense is it "alright" to represent
all conditionals using '→'? Answer: it's just a fact--a plain
old empirical fact--that most of the sound arguments one runs
across in practice can be shown sound using no feature of
conditionals not shared by the material conditional. By
way of illustration, consider the proof of S:

$$
\begin{array}{llll}
1 & (1) & P \rightarrow Q & A \\
2 & (2) & R \ \& \ P & A \\
2 & (3) & P & 2 \ \&E \\
1,2 & (4) & Q & 1,3 \ \text{MPP} \\
1 & (5) & R \ \& \ P \rightarrow Q & 2,4 \ \text{CP}
\end{array}
$$

The conclusion was gotten by CP and so must be construed as a

material conditional. (Thus the provability of S doesn't
establish the soundness of A because the conclusion of that
argument is a subjunctive, not a material, conditional.) The
only fact used about the conditional on line (1), however, is
that if it's true and has a true antecedent, then it also has a
true consequent--a common feature of all conditionals. Accordingly,
for any conditional connective '@', the foregoing proof in effect
establishes the soundness of

$$P \ @ \ Q \vdash R \ \& \ P \rightarrow Q$$

and hence of every argument of that form. Of course, one could
also establish the soundness of such arguments by introducing
'@' into one's formal language, adopting an analog of MPP:

> (MPP*) From A @ B and A, one may derive B
> resting upon the same assumptions as
> the premisses.

and then constructing the following proof:

1	(1)	P @ Q	A
2	(2)	R & P	A
2	(3)	P	2 &E
1, 2	(4)	Q	1, 3 MPP*
1	(5)	R & P $\rightarrow$ Q	2, 4 CP

But why go to all this trouble? We could as well stick with
our original proof and just pretend that '$\rightarrow$' in line (1) represents any kind of conditional we want. Nothing's lost in so
doing, and we have fewer rules (and hence a more elegant
theory of deducibility) with which to contend.

   As I said, most of the sound arguments you meet up with
in practice can be shown sound equivocating (if necessary) on
'$\rightarrow$' in this way. And as long as you pay careful attention to
where CP is employed in your proofs (and hence which occurrences
of '$\rightarrow$' must be construed as material), you should never fall

into the trap of thinking you've proved an argument to be
sound when you haven't. Or you won't, anyway, if you correctly
identified the kinds of conditionals occurring in the argument
and used your rules of derivation properly.

Of course, the trick doesn't <u>always</u> work. It'll sometimes
happen that you need a rule governing a conditional, the effect
of which can't be gotten using MPP, MTT and the rules for 'v', '-',
'&' and the quantifiers. (Argument (a) in this set is a case
in point. The conditionals found in it are subjunctives, and
the best you'll be able to do is show that the conclusion
<u>read as a material conditional</u> follows from the premiss.)
In this case, new connectives are called for in one's formal
language, together with a set of rules governing them.

This latter sort of case typically arises when the
conclusion of your argument is a nonmaterial conditional.
As a practical matter, however, even in these cases one often
needn't worry about having to complicate one's logical theory.
For it often happens that an argument with its conclusion
construed materially will serve the same dialectical function
as that same argument but with its conclusion construed as a
stronger, nonmaterial conditional. (Again, this is because the
only fact about conditionals that frequently interests us is
that if they're true and have a true antecedent, then they
also have a true consequent. Not always; but frequently.)
In such cases, there's no need to prove the soundness of the
original argument. For the dialectical purposes at hand, it'll
suffice to prove the soundness of that same argument but with
its conclusion construed materially--something you can probably
do with the predicate calculus as it stands.

From a practical point of view, then, one represents
all conditionals using '→' because it's handy to do so. With
this in mind, it should now be clear why, for reasoning purposes,
one doesn't also render 'P or Q' as 'P → Q'. It simply wouldn't
work, as there are few, if any, interesting arguments involving

disjunctions that one could prove sound. This is because none
of the analogs of MPP, MTT or CP for 'v', viz.,

> (MPP') From A v B and A, one may derive B
> resting upon the same assumptions as
> the premisses.

> (MTT') From A v B and -B, one may derive -A
> resting upon the same assumptions as
> the premisses.

> (CP') Given a proof of B resting upon A as
> assumption, one may derive A v B resting
> upon the same assumptions as B in its
> derivation from A (apart from A itself).

are sound rules of derivation. Nor, for that matter, are the
analogs of vI and vE for '→', viz.,

> (vI') From A, one may derive A → B (or B → A)
> resting upon the same assumptions as
> the premiss.

> (vE') Given A → B, together with a proof of
> C resting upon A as assumption and a proof
> of C resting upon B as assumption, one may
> derive C. The conclusion rests upon any
> assumption upon which A → B rests, together
> with any assumption upon which C rests in
> its derivation from A (apart from A itself)
> and any assumption upon which C rests in
> its derivation from B (apart from B).

derived rules of the predicate calculus. (In fact, they aren't
even sound.) Indeed, were we to render 'P or Q' as 'P → Q',
not even so simple an argument as:

> Snow is white; therefore, either
> snow is white or grass is green.

could be shown sound using the predicate calculus. For this
would involve proving the sequent-expression:

$$P \vdash P \to Q,$$

which, of course, one can't do. (Why?)

We get away with the convenient fiction that all conditionals are material because often enough it doesn't matter; material and other conditionals share much of their logical behavior. Not so disjunctions and conditionals.

Chapter 3, sec. 3

1   (a) Use 'I' for '...is an Irishman', 'L' for '...likes whiskey', and 'D' for '...is a drinker'. Then the argument is of the form

$$(\exists x)(Ix \ \& \ -Lx), \ (x)(Ix \to Dx) \vdash (\exists x)(Dx \ \& \ -Lx).$$

Prove this sequent to be sound.

(e) Use 'P' for 'Egoism is a moral doctrine', 'R' for '...has the right (according to the Egoist) to do...', 'S' for '...and...are similarly circumstanced' and 'E' for a conjunction of the tenets of Egoism. Then the argument is of the form

$$P \to (E \to (x)(y)(Rxy \to (z)(Szx \to Rzy))),$$
$$(\exists x)(\exists y)(\exists z)(Rxy \ \& \ -Rzy \ \& \ Szx) \vdash E \to -P.$$

```
      1 (1) P → (E → (x)(y)(Rxy → (z)(Szx → Rzy)))    A
      2 (2) E → (∃x)(∃y)(∃z)(Rxy & -Rzy & Szx)        A
      3 (3) E                                          A
      4 (4) P                                          A
   1, 4 (5) E → (x)(y)(Rxy → (z)(Szx → Rzy))          1, 4  MPP
```

1, 3, 4	(6)	(x)(y)(Rxy → (z)(Szx → Rzy))	3, 5	MPP
2, 3	(7)	(∃x)(∃y)(∃z)(Rxy & -Rzy & Szx)	2, 3	MPP
8	(8)	(∃y)(∃z)(Ray & -Rzy & Sza)	A	
9	(9)	(∃z)(Rab & -Rzb & Sza)	A	
10	(10)	Rab & -Rcb & Sca	A	
1, 3, 4	(11)	(y)(Ray → (z)(Sza → Rzy))	6	UE
1, 3, 4	(12)	Rab → (z)(Sza → Rzb)	11	UE
10	(13)	Rab	10	&E
1, 3, 4, 10	(14)	(z)(Sza → Rzb)	12, 13	MPP
1, 3, 4, 10	(15)	Sca → Rcb	14	UE
10	(16)	-Rcb & Sca	10	&E
10	(17)	Sca	16	&E
1, 3, 4, 10	(18)	Rcb	15, 17	MPP
10	(19)	-Rcb	16	&E
1, 3, 4, 10	(20)	Rcb & -Rcb	18, 19	&I
1, 3, 10	(21)	-P	4, 20	RAA
1, 3, 9	(22)	-P	9, 10, 21	EE
1, 3, 8	(23)	-P	8, 9, 22	EE
1, 2, 3	(24)	-P	7, 8, 23	EE
1, 2	(25)	E → -P	2, 24	CP

This is a complex proof, but one which will repay careful study. It's a nice illustration of the proper use of EE and underscores just how complex an innocent-looking English argument can be.

Chapter 3, sec. 5

1   (a) Use 'L' for '...likes...'. Then the argument is of the form

$$(\exists x)(y)-Lxy, \quad (x)(y)(-Lyy \rightarrow -Lxy) \vdash (\exists x)(y)-Lyx.$$

1	(1)	(∃x)(y)-Lxy	A
2	(2)	(x)(y)(-Lyy → -Lxy)	A

3	(3) (y)-Lay	A
3	(4) -Laa	3 UE
2	(5) (y)(-Lyy → -Lby)	2 UE
2	(6) -Laa → -Lba	5 UE
2, 3	(7) -Lba	4, 6 MPP
2, 3	(8) (y)-Lya	7 UI
2, 3	(9) (∃x)(y)-Lyx	8 EI
1, 2	(10) (∃x)(y)-Lyx	1, 3, 9 EE

(d) Use 'm' for 'Lodge', 'n' for 'Jain' and 'B' for '...can do...better than...can do...'. Then the argument is of the form

$$(\exists x)(y)Bnxmy, \; -(\exists x)Bmxmx, \; (x)(y)(z)(Bmxny \; \& $$
$$Bnymz \rightarrow Bmxmz) \vdash -(x)Bmxnx,$$

the third premiss being implicit in what's said explicitly.

1	(1) (∃x)(y)Bnxmy	A
2	(2) -(∃x)Bmxmx	A
3	(3) (x)(y)(z)(Bmxny & Bnymz → Bmxmz)	A
4	(4) (x)Bmxnx	A
5	(5) (y)Bnamy	A
5	(6) Bnama	5 UE
4	(7) Bmana	4 UE
4, 5	(8) Bmana & Bnama	6, 7 &I
3	(9) (y)(z)(Bmany & Bnymz → Bmamz)	3 UE
3	(10) (z)(Bmana & Bnamz → Bmamz)	9 UE
3	(11) Bmana & Bnama → Bmama	10 UE
3, 4, 5	(12) Bmama	8, 11 MPP
3, 4, 5	(13) (∃x)Bmxmx	12 EI
1, 3, 4	(14) (∃x)Bmxmx	1, 5, 13 EE
1, 2, 3, 4	(15) (∃x)Bmxmx & -(∃x)Bmxmx	2, 14 &I
1, 2, 3	(16) -(x)Bmxnx	4, 15 RAA

(e) In saying that failure to perform a certain action

would be unlawful, Hobbes evidently means that such failure
would result in one's disobeying the law of nature. Accordingly,
if we use 'R' for '...is a ruler', 'N' for '...obeys the law of
nature', 'M' for '...does everything possible to protect the
subjects of...', 'S' for '...sends out spies, etc.' and 'L'
for '...acts lawfully in sending out spies, etc.', we can
take the argument to be of the form

$$(x)(Rx \rightarrow (Nx \rightarrow Mxx)), \quad (x)(Rx \rightarrow (Mxx \rightarrow Sx)),$$
$$(x)((Nx \rightarrow Mxx) \ \& \ (Mxx \rightarrow Sx) \rightarrow Lx) \vdash (x)(Rx \rightarrow Lx \ \&$$
$$(-Sx \rightarrow -Nx)).$$

The third premiss is only implicit in what Hobbes says, but
is a plausible "deontic" principle which he is clearly endorsing:
Any means necessary to achieve something lawfully required is
itself legally permitted.

[The second conditionals in the first two premisses
(and hence also the first two conditionals in the third premiss)
were almost certainly meant by Hobbes to be stronger than just
material conditionals. No harm is done, however, in representing
them all with '$\rightarrow$' as the only assumption about those conditionals
used in the proof of the foregoing sequent-expression is that
they satisfy MPP--a rule satisfied by all conditionals. By
contrast, the two conditionals in the conclusion must be
construed as material since they will be introduced into the
proof by CP. (See pp. 83-9 above.) Hobbes may have had a
stronger conclusion in mind, but this is about the best we
can do with the resources you have at hand.]

Chapter 4, sec. 1

2   (d) Let e be any arbitrary name not appearing in
C $\rightarrow$ (v)A(v) or in any assumption listed in the box. [How does
one know there is such a term?]

```
                              .
                              .
                              .
              ┌─────┐  (i)  C → (v)A(v)
              └─────┘        .
                              .
                              .
         j  (j)  C                          A
                              .
                              .
                              .
    j, ┌─────┐  (k)   (v)A(v)              i, j  MPP
    j, ┌─────┐  (k + 1)  A(e)              k  UE
       ┌─────┐  (k + 2)  C → A(e)          j, k + 1  CP
       ┌─────┐  (k + 3)  (v)(C → A(v))     k + 2  UI
```

[Notice that e had to be picked as it was so as to ensure (i)
that one <u>could</u> use UI at line (k + 3) and (ii) that C → A(v) is
what results from replacing all occurrences of e in C → A(e) by
v, so that (v)(C → A(v)) is what one gets when UI is used. The
requirement that v not appear in C was necessary again to ensure
that UI was properly used--remember, v has to be a variable
not appearing in C → A(e). (It doesn't appear in A(e), of
course, because A(e) is the result of replacing all occurrences
of v in A(v) by e.)]

Chapter 4, sec. 2

1   (a) Read 'F' as '...is French' and 'G' as '...is European'.

     (e) Read 'F' as '...had...as a mother'.

Chapter 4, sec. 3

1   (c)   1 (1) (x)(x = a)   A
              2 (2) -(b = c)   A
              1 (3) b = a   1 UE
              1 (4) c = a   1 UE
```
```

```
      1 (5)  b = c                    3, 4 SI Ex. 4.3.1(c)
   1, 2 (6)  (b = c) & -(b = c)       2, 5 &I
      1 (7)  --(b = c)                2, 6 RAA
      1 (8)  b = c                    7 DN
      1 (9)  (y)(b = y)               8 UI
      1 (10) (x)(y)(x = y)            9 UI
```

2   (b) Use 'C' for '...is a cat', 'F' for '...was found at...' and 'a' for 'Barney's'.

   (∃x)(∃y)(∃z)(-(x = y) & -(x = z) & -(y = z) &
   Cx & Cy & Cz & Fxa & Fya & Fza & (w)(Cw & Fwa →
   w = x v w = y v w = z))

   (d) (x)(∃y)(x = y)

   (f) Use 'a' for 'Clyde', 'b' for 'Sue', 'c' for 'Harry' 'T' for '...is taller than...' and 'P' for '...is a player'.

   Tab & Tac & (x)(Px & -(x = b) & -(x = c) → -Tax)

   (h) Use 'a' for 'me', 'b' for 'Rudolph' and 'T' for '...was there'.

   (x)(Tx ↔ x = a v x = b)

3   (b) Use 'a' for 'Sue', 'b' for 'Carol', 'c' for 'Bill', 'd' for 'Ralph', 'E' for '...extended such-and-such efforts', 'M' for '...made it' and 'D' for '...deserves better'. Then the argument is of the form

   -Ea → (x)(Mx → x = b), Mc, Md, -(b = c),
              -(b = d), (x)(Ex → Dx) ⊢ Da.

Prove this sequent to be sound.

4   (a) Use 'P' for '...is a President', 'C' for '...is

Commander-in-Chief', 'F' for '...is a peanut farmer', 'G'
for '...farms in Georgia' and 'B' for '...is better known than
any other peanut farmer in Georgia'. Then the argument is of
the form

$$(\exists x)((y)(Py \leftrightarrow y = x) \ \& \ Cx), \ (\exists x)((y)(Fy \ \& \ Gy \ \& \ By \leftrightarrow y = x) \ \& \ Cx), \ (x)(y)(Cx \ \& \ Cy \rightarrow x = y) \vdash (\exists x)((y)(Py \leftrightarrow y = x) \ \& \ Fx).$$

1	(1)	$(\exists x)((y)(Py \leftrightarrow y = x) \ \& \ Cx)$	A
2	(2)	$(\exists x)((y)(Fy \ \& \ Gy \ \& \ By \leftrightarrow y = x) \ \& \ Cx)$	A
3	(3)	$(x)(y)(Cx \ \& \ Cy \rightarrow x = y)$	A
4	(4)	$(y)(Py \leftrightarrow y = a) \ \& \ Ca$	A
5	(5)	$(y)(Fy \ \& \ Gy \ \& \ By \leftrightarrow y = b) \ \& \ Cb$	A
3	(6)	$(y)(Ca \ \& \ Cy \rightarrow a = y)$	3 UE
3	(7)	$Ca \ \& \ Cb \rightarrow a = b$	6 UE
4	(8)	Ca	4 &E
5	(9)	Cb	5 &E
4, 5	(10)	$Ca \ \& \ Cb$	8, 9 &I
3, 4, 5	(11)	$a = b$	7, 10 MPP
5	(12)	$(y)(Fy \ \& \ Gy \ \& \ By \leftrightarrow y = b)$	5 &E
5	(13)	$Fa \ \& \ Ga \ \& \ Ba \leftrightarrow a = b$	12 UE
3, 4, 5	(14)	$Fa \ \& \ Ga \ \& \ Ba$	11, 13 SI(S) Ex. 1.4.1(a)
3, 4, 5	(15)	Fa	14 &E
4	(16)	$(y)(Py \leftrightarrow y = a)$	4 &E
3, 4, 5	(17)	$(y)(Py \leftrightarrow y = a) \ \& \ Fa$	15, 16 &I
3, 4, 5	(18)	$(\exists x)((y)(Py \leftrightarrow y = x) \ \& \ Fx)$	17 EI
1, 3, 5	(19)	$(\exists x)((y)(Py \leftrightarrow y = x) \ \& \ Fx)$	1, 4, 18 EE
1, 2, 3	(20)	$(\exists x)((y)(Py \leftrightarrow y = x) \ \& \ Fx)$	2, 5, 19 EE

(c) Use 'B' for '...is a barber' and 'S' for '...shaved
...'. Then the argument is of the form

$$\vdash - (\exists x)(\exists y)((z)((w)(Szw \leftrightarrow -Sww) \ \& \ Bz \leftrightarrow z = y) \ \& \ x = y).$$

```
  1  (1)  (∃x)(∃y)((z)((w)(Szw ↔ -Sww) &      A
           Bz ↔ z = y) & x = y)

  2  (2)  (∃y)((z)((w)(Szw ↔ -Sww) &           A
           Bz ↔ z = y) & a = y)

  3  (3)  (z)((w)(Szw ↔ -Sww) & Bz ↔           A
           z = b) & a = b

  3  (4)  (z)((w)(Szw ↔ -Sww) & Bz ↔           3 &E
           z = b)

  3  (5)  (w)(Sbw ↔ -Sww) & Bb ↔ b = b         4 UE

  3  (6)  ((w)(Sbw ↔ -Sww) & Bb → b = b)       5 Df. ↔
           & (b = b → (w)(Sbw ↔ -Sww) &
           Bb)

  3  (7)  b = b → (w)(Sbw ↔ -Sww) & Bb         6 &E

     (8)  b = b                                =I

  3  (9)  (w)(Sbw ↔ -Sww) & Bb                 7, 8 MPP

  3 (10)  (w)(Sbw ↔ -Sww)                      9 &E

  3 (11)  Sbb ↔ -Sbb                           10 UE

    (12)  Sbb v -Sbb                           TI(S) 44

 13 (13)  Sbb                                  A

3, 13 (14)  -Sbb                               11, 13  SI(S) 25

3, 13 (15)  Sbb & -Sbb                         13, 14 &I

 16 (16)  -Sbb                                 A

3, 16 (17)  Sbb                                11, 16  SI(S) Ex.
                                               1.4.1(a)

3, 16 (18)  Sbb & -Sbb                         16, 17 &I

  3 (19)  Sbb & -Sbb                           12, 13, 15, 16,
                                               18 vE

1, 3 (20)  Sbb & -Sbb & (∃x)(∃y)((z)((w)       1, 19  &I
           (Szw ↔ -Sww) & Bz ↔ z = y)
           & x = y)

1, 3 (21)  Sbb & -Sbb                          20 &E

  3 (22)  -(∃x)(∃y)((z)((w)(Szw ↔ -Sww)        1, 21  RAA
           & Bz ↔ z = y) & x = y)

  2 (23)  -(∃x)(∃y)((z)((w)(Szw ↔ -Sww)        2, 3, 22 EE
           & Bz ↔ z = y) & x = y)

  1 (24)  -(∃x)(∃y)((z)((w)(Szw ↔ -Sww)        1, 2, 23 EE
           & Bz ↔ z = y) & x = y)

  1 (25)  (∃x)(∃y)((z)((w)(Szw ↔ -Sww) &       1, 24  &I
           Bz ↔ z = y) & x = y) & -(∃x)
           (∃y)((z)((w)(Szw ↔ -Sww) & Bz
           ↔ z = y) & x = y)
```

(26) $-(\exists x)(\exists y)((z)((w)(Szw \leftrightarrow -Sww) \& \quad$ 1, 25 RAA
          $Bz \leftrightarrow z = y) \& x = y)$

Glimpses Beyond

1   (b)   1 (1) $\Box P \lor \Box Q$ A

          2 (2) $\Box P$ A

          3 (3) P A

          3 (4) $P \lor Q$ 3 vI

             (5) $P \rightarrow P \lor Q$ 3, 4 CP

             (6) $\Box(P \rightarrow P \lor Q)$ 5 RN

          2 (7) $\Box(P \lor Q)$ 2, 6 NC

          8 (8) $\Box Q$ A

          9 (9) Q A

          9 (10) $P \lor Q$ 9 vI

             (11) $Q \rightarrow P \lor Q$ 9, 10 CP

             (12) $\Box(Q \rightarrow P \lor Q)$ 11 RN

          8 (13) $\Box(P \lor Q)$ 8, 12 NC

          1 (14) $\Box(P \lor Q)$ 1, 2, 7, 8, 13 vE

     (c)   1 (1) $\Box P \& \Box Q$ A

          2 (2) P A

          3 (3) Q A

        2, 3 (4) $P \& Q$ 2, 3 &I

          2 (5) $Q \rightarrow P \& Q$ 3, 4 CP

             (6) $P \rightarrow (Q \rightarrow P \& Q)$ 2, 5 CP

             (7) $\Box(P \rightarrow (Q \rightarrow P \& Q))$ 6 RN

          1 (8) $\Box P$ 1 &E

          1 (9) $\Box(Q \rightarrow P \& Q)$ 7, 8 NC

          1 (10) $\Box Q$ 1 &E

          1 (11) $\Box(P \& Q)$ 9, 10 NC

[The other half of (c) is similar.]

     (e)   1 (1) $\Box-(P \rightarrow \Box P)$ A

          2 (2) $-(P \rightarrow \Box P)$ A

```
      2 (3)  P & -□P                              2 SI(S) Ex. 2.2.5(g)
        (4)  -(P → □P) → (P & -□P)                2, 3 CP
        (5)  □(-(P → □P) → (P & -□P))             4 RN
      1 (6)  □(P & - P)                           1, 5 NC
      1 (7)  □P & □-□P                            6 SI(S) Ex. (c)
      1 (8)  □P                                   7 &E
      1 (9)  □-□P                                 7 &E
     1 (10)  -□P                                  9 □E
     1 (11)  □P & -□P                             8, 10 &I
       (12)  -□-(P → □P)                          1, 11 RAA


(f)  1 (1)  -□-(P v Q)                            A
     2 (2)  -(-□-P v -□-Q)                        A
     2 (3)  --□-P & --□-Q                         2 SI(S) Ex. 1.5.1(f)
     2 (4)  --□-P                                 3 &E
     2 (5)  □-P                                   4 DN
     2 (6)  --□-Q                                 3 &E
     2 (7)  □-Q                                   6 DN
     8 (8)  -P & -Q                               A
     8 (9)  -(P v Q)                              8 SI Ex. 1.5.1(f)
      (10)  (-P & -Q) → -(P v Q)                  8, 9 CP
      (11)  □((-P & -Q) → -(P v Q))               10 RN
    2 (12)  □-P & □-Q                             5, 7 &I
    2 (13)  □(-P & -Q)                            12 SI(S) Ex. (c)
    2 (14)  □-(P v Q)                             11, 13 NC
 1, 2 (15)  □-(P v Q) & -□-(P v Q)                1, 14 &I
    1 (16)  --(-□-P v -□-Q)                       2, 15 RAA
    1 (17)  -□-P v -□-Q                           16 DN
```